Eng. by John Sartain. Phil?

Yrs Very Truly
John M. Lowrie

THE

PROPHET ELISHA.

JOHN McLOWRIE, D.D.,

AUTHOR OF

"ESTHER AND HER TIMES," "ADAM AND HIS TIMES," "THE HEBREW LAW-GIVER," "A WEEK WITH JESUS," "THE TRANSLATED PROPHET," ETC.

TO WHICH IS PREFIXED

A MEMOIR OF THE AUTHOR.

BY THE

REV. WILLIAM D. HOWARD, D.D.,

PASTOR OF THE SECOND PRESBYTERIAN CHURCH OF PITTSBURG, PA.

PHILADELPHIA:

PRESBYTERIAN BOARD OF PUBLICATION,

No. 821 CHESTNUT STREET.

WESTCOTT & THOMSON,
Stereotypers, Philada.

CONTENTS.

MEMOIR OF DR. LOWRIE.

BY THE

REV. W. D. HOWARD, D.D.

THE REV. JOHN M. LOWRIE, D.D., the author of the following volume, as also of several others published by the Board of Publication, was born in the city of Pittsburg on the 16th of July, 1817. His father, the Hon. Matthew B. Lowrie, was a native of Scotland, but immigrated to this country early in life. The family settled in Western Pennsylvania, where, owing to their intelligence, integrity and energy, they exerted a wide and wholesome influence. The father of the subject of this memoir was for many years a magistrate, first of the borough and afterward of the city of Pittsburg, the duties of which office he discharged with eminent ability and fidelity. At an early period of life he became an avowed follower of the Lord Jesus Christ, and from May, 1821, until his lamented death in 1851, with the exception of a few years when he was absent from the city, he was an active, useful and influential elder in the Second Presbyterian Church of Pittsburg. To this faithful servant of Christ belongs the chief honour of founding the first Sabbath-school, on the plan of the celebrated Robert Raikes, west of the Allegheny Mountains. Mr. M. B. Lowrie was twice married. His first wife, and the mother of all his children, was Miss Sarah Anderson. She was a woman of unusual vigour of intellect and rare decision and energy of character. She had much to do in training and disciplining a large family, who are, in no small degree, indebted to her wisdom and piety for the honourable and useful places many of them have been permitted to occupy in society. One of her sons became the chief justice of Pennsylvania; another was an eminent physician; a third, the subject of this brief biographical sketch, one of the most learned, laborious and useful ministers of his generation.

Mr. Lowrie's early education, though confined to those branches of learning designed to fit him for secular employments, was careful and thorough. His purpose was to devote himself to mercantile pursuits, and at an early age he entered the service of a brother-in-law, then at the head of a large and flourishing establishment. He had unusual qualifications for this walk of life, and, had he devoted himself to it, would doubtless have attained both eminence and fortune. But he sacrificed his pleasant position and flattering prospects to a conviction that he was called to a nobler, but by no means so lucrative, a sphere of action.

When he was about seventeen years of age he became more deeply interested in the subject of his personal salvation than he had been before, and in November, 1834, he made a public profession of religion, uniting himself with the Second Presbyterian Church of Pittsburg. From this time his mind seems to have been so absorbed with thoughts of the ministry that, with little further delay, with the full consent of his parents and friends, he relinquished his business and entered upon a course of preparatory study for this holy calling. He entered the preparatory department of Jefferson College, and continued in that institution till the close of his second collegiate year, when he transferred his relation to Lafayette College, entering that institution at the beginning of the Junior year in the fall of 1838, and graduating with distinction in the fall of 1840.

Mr. Lowrie's collegiate course was marked by unusual industry and fidelity. His love of learning was intense: he was not satisfied to confine himself to the prescribed studies of the college course, but was disposed, both in languages and mathematics, to range over a much wider field. A classmate thus speaks of these pursuits: "He read outside of the regular course, while at Easton, Homer (Iliad and Odyssey), Virgil, and several of the plays of Sophocles and Euripides (perhaps others that I do not now recall), in the original, and amused himself by putting some of them into a metrical translation." Another says: "One vacation was spent, when at home from Easton, in prosecuting mathematical studies with a former classmate beyond the course" either in Jefferson or Lafayette.

But though thus devoted to learning, he found time for social intercourse, and especially for Christian labour. "His whole influence," says one, "was on the side of *right;* and yet he was a very cheerful and witty companion, and, whilst he adhered strictly to principle, he was far removed from moroseness." And another: "His habits were eminently devout, though with no parade or ostentation, and no sanctimoniousness." And still another: "There could be no mistake about his Christian character; he was earnest, ardent, zealous, and always ready to 'stand up for Jesus.'" While at Easton "he was active in Sunday-schools and other evangelistic operations, walking back in the country two or three miles to a neglected and ignorant population, where he, with other students, whom he interested in the cause, maintained a Sabbath-school; and by the teachers' meetings, which he conducted, he continued to make it of as much benefit to them as to their pupils." But it was, perhaps, among his fellow-students he accomplished the greatest amount of good. An eminent servant of Christ, who now occupies one of the most important positions in the Church, thus writes: "It was by his Christian fidelity and his earnest persuasions and prayers that I was led to seek a personal interest in the Saviour's love." And there can be no doubt he laboured thus with others, and possibly with like success.

On the 5th of November, 1840, the first day of the fall session, he entered the Theological Seminary at Princeton, and pursued the full course of study in that institution, though he left it a short time before graduating. In the seminary as in college his habits were extremely regular, and his devotion to study amounted almost to a passion. One of his fellow-students says: "He stood high among his classmates in point of scholarship in every department of study. His habits, temper and whole deportment produced a conviction that his piety was genuine and profound, and that the love of Christ was the governing power in all he said or did."

On the 5th of October, 1841, he was taken under the

care of the Presbytery of Newton as a candidate for the holy ministry, and was licensed by that presbytery on the 27th of April, 1842. It was his purpose, cherished for a long time, to spend his life in the work of a foreign missionary. His attention at one time seems to have been directed to Africa, and afterward to India, but the feeble health of near relatives obliged him to relinquish his purpose in both instances. Had his design been carried out, and his life spared for some years, there can be no doubt he would have ranked, like others of his name and kindred, among the ablest, most devoted and most successful missionaries our country has furnished. But it was wisely ordered otherwise. The theatre of his noble lifework was to be his native land.

In April, 1843, Mr. Lowrie was married to Miss Hetty Dusenbury, with whom he had become acquainted while a student at Easton. This most estimable lady was the faithful and affectionate partner of his life, and now, with four children, survives him. About this time he was called to the churches of Blairstown and Knowlton, in Warren county, New Jersey, and was ordained and installed there on the 18th of October, 1843. With the diligence which characterized him through life, he laboured in this field until the 1st of April, 1845, when, on account of feeble health, he sought a dissolution of the relation. He was dismissed on the 27th of April, 1846, to join the Presbytery of Steubenville, having in the mean time been called to the church in Wellsville, Ohio. He remained in Wellsville, the church prospering under his ministry, until April, 1850, when he was called to Lancaster, Ohio. There, too, his faithful and assiduous efforts were blessed by the Head of the Church, and after labouring for about six years in that place, he was translated to Fort Wayne, Indiana, the last and most important theatre of his ministerial labours. He was installed there in November, 1856, and entered at once with great earnestness and zeal upon the duties of his office. He felt that at length he had found an appropriate sphere of action. The city was comparatively new, but promised to be of rapid and substantial growth. In the midst of a large, increasing and intelligent community, his cultivated intellect and vast stores of biblical and theological knowledge might be expected to produce most happy fruits. Always systematic and thorough in his studies, wise in laying his plans and prompt in executing them, when he entered upon his work in Fort Wayne he marked out for himself a scheme of labour unusual for its breadth and completeness, and then pursued it with an ardour, zeal, self-devotion—ay, and self-sacrifice—to which there are, perhaps, few parallels. There was nothing spasmodic in his efforts, no attempt at display, nothing done for effect. There was in his work a steady and beautiful development, the result of an intellectual and spiritual life of unusual vigour. He was in the prime of his days and the full maturity of his powers. One of the members of his session, speaking of his efforts, says: "He applied himself to his Master's work with untiring labour. His labours were too abundant; he worked beyond his physical ability. His interest in and devotion to the spread of the gospel, the building up of the Church here and elsewhere, were the guiding stars of every action and every thought.

'Christ and his cross was all his theme.'

Bodily labor, mental effort and pecuniary means were all laid upon the altar to further the interests of Christ's kingdom." Such labours, and such a labourer, it is reasonable to suppose, would be much blessed. At his installation there were on the roll of the church one hundred and seventy-one names. At the close of his ministry, as also of his life, a period of less than eleven years, three of which were years of suffering and declining health—years in which, unless inspired by an energy, hopefulness and love for the Master's cause of very rare occurrence, no one would have worked at all—notwithstanding all the changes by death and removal, there were three hundred and eighteen names, making it the largest church in the Synod of Northern Indiana. On three several occasions there were precious outpourings of the Spirit among his people. The first was in 1859, when thirty-three persons were added to the church on profession of their faith; the second in 1864, when there were eighteen; and the third in 1866, when there were forty-six. The whole period of his ministry was something over twenty-four years, and there are probably but few who in that time have done so much work and done it so well. These are some of the principal events in the life of the Rev. John M. Lowrie—a man distinguished for the beauty and symmetry of his character, and remarkable alike for his learning and piety, and for his industry and success in the holy ministry.

Dr. Lowrie was a man of much more than ordinary natural gifts. His intellect was clear and vigorous, his judgment sound, his apprehension quick and his memory retentive. He had a happy faculty both of acquiring and retaining knowledge. Nor was he by any means deficient in imagination. Most apposite and beautiful illustrations are found liberally scattered through his works; besides which he is the author of a number of hymns which have a high degree of poetic merit. But the logical predominated over the imaginative in his mind. He excelled in systematic arrangement, clear statement, together with forcible and conclusive argument. Even in college he was an admirable essayist and debater, and fully the equal of those among his fellow-students who since have shown themselves, in various walks of professional life, to be men of rare ability. These qualities were exhibited both in his preaching and in his published works. If he did not possess brilliant parts, he possessed parts which were far better. He was lucid, forcible, compact, argumentative. He was not the man to sacrifice a thought, much less a truth, to an antithesis or a trope. His chief aim was, not to please the fancy, but to convince the judgment, arouse the conscience and affect the heart. And to accomplish these ends his well-balanced, well-furnished, earnest and logical mind was well fitted.

The surroundings of his childhood and youth were well adapted to develop a noble character. Allusion has already been made to his home, to the intelligence and piety of his parents and the social position of his family. The community in which he lived exerted a happy influence on his young mind. There was in Pittsburg sin enough, no doubt —enough intemperance, profanity and Sabbath-breaking— enough rudeness and lawlessness. But nevertheless society there had a healthy moral tone. It was a Scotch-Irish community in great part, and they are a people who have great respect for the gospel, the Sabbath, the sanctuary and its ordinances. They were a people remarkable for their industrious habits, their commercial integrity and their freedom from extravagant customs. But besides this, owing to the soundness of his judgment and the early maturity of his character, when very young he was engaged in active business. He enjoyed what few of his co-workers in the ministry do—a thorough business training. This was of great advantage to him through life. It enabled him not only to "guide his affairs with discretion," and to give sound advice in regard to the secularities of the congregations he served, but fitted him to discharge with unusual ability many duties which devolve on members of church courts. He had few equals, and perhaps not a superior, in the whole Church as a member of an ecclesiastical assembly. Few could preside with more dignity and skill over a deliberative body; few were more forcible, yet more courteous in debate; and few were more efficient as a member of a committee.

Eminent spirituality was characteristic of him. There was no parade or display about his piety; few men had a deeper abhorrence of such things. Having maturely considered the doctrines of our holy religion, he was fully satisfied of their truth. To use his own language on his dying bed: "I have examined all the historical connections of Christ; the necessity of a Mediator and Redeemer; the time and circumstances of all things connected with the subject of salvation through Christ. I feel happy that I have been able to examine all the truths of religion so thoroughly, and come to such conclusions that I am enabled to rejoice in Christ and no other. I feel that he is all-sufficient to present me faultless before his Father." And yet his religion was not a religion of the intellect alone. His affections also were profoundly interested. He loved his Saviour, loved his cause, loved his service, loved his people. He was a man of much religious meditation, of much prayer —one who was much with Jesus. One of the works he published bears the touching and beautiful title, "A Week with Jesus." It was prepared for the press—if not in considerable part written—during his protracted illness; and he often wrote to Dr. Schenck, the Secretary of the Board of Publication, while making arrangements for its issue, expressing in "very earnest and tender terms the benefits his own soul had received while handling the precious truths contained in it." To which Dr. Schenck adds: "He seems to have been himself much with Jesus, and to have been drinking in of his instructions and his spirit."

His preparation for the work of the ministry was more than usually complete. Though he commenced his classical studies later in life than some do, he pursued them with such assiduity that he reached a higher degree of perfection than most. His scholarship was of a high grade. His attainments in the classics and mathematics, his acquaintance with history, science and general literature, were extensive and accurate. Few in the ministry, perhaps, have made themselves so familiar with poetry, both classical and English. The same winter he read Homer and Virgil in the originals he read "Paradise Lost," thus perusing at the same time the three great epics of Greece, Italy and England. Of all the British poets, if we except the hymnologists, for whom he seems to have had a special affection, Milton, we presume, was his favourite. His capacious memory—a memory which, in his biblical studies, enabled him to dispense with the use of a concordance—was stored with the choicest passages of these authors, and he often happily called them to his aid in elucidating and enforcing truth. But it was in the department of theology that his greatest attainments were made. His theological course, as has already been stated, was thorough; and through the whole course of his ministry his study of this science was pursued to a far greater extent than is usual. Nor did he confine himself to the theology, so rich and abundant, of his native tongue, but had recourse to the vast stores which are locked up in the classical languages. Professor Green, of Princeton, a most competent judge, in writing to the author of this Memoir, says of him: "I doubt if any of our ministry, not filling professorships, were as profoundly read in Latin theology."

But notwithstanding these large general attainments, he made the most careful special preparation for the pulpit. Scarcely could any one be more industrious, conscientious and prayerful in this matter than he. The whole structure and habit of his mind led to this. He did not feel that it was sufficient to harangue a congregation. There was nothing in his nature, especially in his nature as sanctified by the Divine Spirit, to lead him to make a display of his talents or his learning; he was too earnest and sincere a man for any such mockery. He felt himself called upon to instruct his people—to instruct them systematically; to instruct them not only in the doctrines, but in the historical portions of the Bible. Hence his "*Adam and his Times*," his "*Esther and her Times*," his "*Hebrew Lawgiver*," his "*Week with Jesus*," his "*Translated Prophet*," his "*Prophet Elisha*," and the like—all of which, or nearly all, went through the pulpit. This method gave a delightful variety to his ministrations, and made them especially interesting and profitable. And in all this there was nothing irksome to him. He loved this careful, thorough, systematic work; it was in harmony with his nature, and easy from long-established habit. He said to one of his elders on his deathbed "that his heart had always been in his work." How immeasurably better is this plan of pulpit ministration than the desultory method in which many pastors indulge! How pleasant is this to the labourer himself, how beneficial to a congregation, and how worthy the imitation of all engaged in preaching the gospel!

From this it is plain he was a man of pre-eminent industry. He was, indeed, a most persistent worker. Work was a pleasure to him. He was always in advance of his work. It was never with him, as with so many of his brethren, "from hand to mouth." He always worked more than the circumstances demanded. It was so in college; it was so in the seminary; it was so in his pastorate; it was so in regard to his works for the press. The pulpit never pushed him—he always had sermons in advance; the press never pushed him—he always had books in advance. At his death he had two manuscript volumes in the hands of the Board of Publication, and even these did not exhaust his labours in this department. This industry was one chief cause of his unusual success. All his rare talent and ample preparation would have availed but little had he been a less earnest and constant worker. And in this he is worthy the imitation of all his brethren, young and old.

His moral courage and firmness of purpose were frequently put to the test, and he was found to possess these, as so many other excellent qualities, in a high degree. He was as far removed as possible from harshness or obstinacy. But when principle was involved, and when he had carefully made up his mind on any question of duty—any question in politics, morals or religion—he was as firm as the hills which girdle his native city. He ever earnestly and fearlessly opposed wrong-doing, no matter who were its agents. He had no fear of the face of man, and was just as ready, if, indeed, not more ready, to grapple with the advocates of wrong or the assailants of right when they occupied high social or civil positions, or were distinguished for their ability or wealth, as when they belonged to the baser sort.

In all the relations of life, as son, brother, husband, pastor, friend, citizen, he was exemplary. He was a sincere, conscientious, upright, devout man. In the recent national struggle with armed rebellion he stood firmly by the government. He had not a shadow of doubt as to the righteousness of the national cause, and was ever full of hope as to the successful termination of the war. With other humane and Christian men, he deplored the necessity of the conflict, but he believed, through the overruling providence of God in removing slavery and its concomitant evils, it would result in good to the country and the world. He regarded it as a special privilege to be permitted to live and to take part in the stirring and most important events of his time. But he shone brightest as a Christian man and a Christian minister. He was wholly devoted to Christ and his cause. "For him to live was Christ." He studied Christ; he preached Christ; he imitated Christ; he had much communion with his divine Master, and was never so happy as when labouring with tongue and pen to promote his cause. The members of that beloved congregation in the midst of which he spent the last years of his life can bear witness how gentle and yet how firm, how tender and yet how true, how loving and yet how faithful, how benevolent and yet how discreet, how devout and yet how cheerful he was. His beautiful life was daily before their eyes, and was as instructive as his rare and unvaried labours.

As a preacher Dr. Lowrie was not, as the phrase is now by many understood, an eloquent man. His voice was not good, and he was indifferent to the graces of manner. He was too quiet, too undemonstrative, too sparing of gesture, too meditative to be classed among pulpit orators. Indeed, for very much of what goes under the name of eloquence he could scarcely conceal his contempt. Not more ready was the poet himself than he to say:

"Avaunt all attitude and stare,
And start theatric, practiced at the glass!
I seek divine simplicity in him
Who handles things divine; and all besides,
Though learned with labour, and though much admired
By curious eyes and judgments ill informed,
To me is odious."

In another passage of the same poem we have his portrait so admirably drawn that the inclination to reproduce it cannot be resisted. Emphatically he was

> "Simple, grave, sincere;
> In doctrine uncorrupt; in language plain,
> And plain in manner; decent, solemn, chaste,
> And natural in gesture: much impressed
> Himself, as conscious of his awful charge,
> And anxious mainly that the flock he feeds
> May feel it too; affectionate in look
> And tender in address, as well becomes
> A messenger of grace to guilty men."

His published works partake very much of the character of his discourses. Indeed, in the main they are his discourses recast, and yet they do not afford a complete idea of his method as a sermonizer. In these works he confined himself to historical portions of Scripture, for which he had a special fondness, and from which he had a rare faculty of deriving practical instruction. His writings are characterized by clear statement rather than novel views; by a perspicuous rather than an ornate style; by affectionate appeals to the heart rather than attempts to please the fancy. They are methodical, original and earnest. His descriptions are graphic, his figures animated, his diction vigorous, his doctrines sound, though, as he wrote for the unlearned, not expressed in the language of the schools, and his aim the instruction and salvation of his readers.

But there was nothing more beautiful nor more instructive than his death. His illness was protracted and painful. When at length he was obliged to suspend his labours and seek relief, he visited his native hills, and no doubt, had his disease not been too deeply seated for any human remedies to reach, rest from his exhausting toils and the pure air of that healthful region would have restored him. This failing, at the urgent solicitation of anxious friends he went abroad, hoping to be benefited by foreign travel. To a man of his culture and tastes this was pleasant not only, but profitable, and, in some little degree, beneficial to his health. But all efforts failed fully to accomplish what was desired. If there was any relief, it was only temporary. Disease had taken too deep a hold to be shaken off. But neither distance nor disease could banish his flock from his mind, or induce him to relinquish his efforts for their edification. His plans of usefulness, his habits of thought, his habits of work went with him, so that in the intervals of travel he was engaged in writing discourses he purposed to deliver when restored to them. One which he had proposed to preach immediately upon his return he had finished, when, on a Sabbath morning, in the city of Calvin, he repaired to the room of two pious young relatives, in whose company he travelled, for the purpose of reading it to them. He commenced, but, before he had proceeded far, his emotion choked his utterance, and thoughts of his family, his home and his flock made him weep like a child.

Upon his return from Europe he partially resumed his labours, but never with sufficient health to pursue them with safety or vigour. At length the insidious disease which had so long preyed upon his system assumed a new form, and he was laid upon the bed from which he never rose. Faithful friends and constant attendants—one an elder in his church as also his family physician, and another member of his session—have furnished some of his last words.

He spoke of his work. This seems scarcely to have been absent from his thoughts. There was much he yet purposed to do—much he "yet wanted to do." He desired to pursue his "systematic discussions in the pulpit" and to prepare other volumes for the press. But he had scarcely uttered the words when he checked himself, saying, "I give these things into the hands of God. Should I live twenty years longer, it would to me probably appear the same. God knows best when each man's work is done." Then, like Paul, he was ready to say, "I have finished my course."

The prosperity of the cause of Christ among his people occupied much of his thoughts. He was deeply interested in a mission enterprise they had commenced at his suggestion, with the ultimate purpose of organizing a second church in Fort Wayne. He spoke affectionately of the brother having charge of it, and felt assured, as it was begun under the evident smile of Providence, it would prosper. His own congregation, for which he expressed the deepest solicitude, he committed to God, expressing the hope that no root of bitterness would spring up among them, and that in choosing a pastor they would be led to choose one after God's own heart. He prayed most earnestly that "God the Father would bless the Church." He was very solicitous that the utmost harmony should continue among its officers; "that no discordant element or thought would spring up among them, but that harmony and good-will might characterize all" their actions. It was his desire that they should "study well the interests of the church, and especially its peace in all things." "May they be united," was his prayer, "in the bonds of brotherly love and friendship, working together for the good of God's Church." Just before his departure his mind again reverted to his people, and among the last objects for which he audibly prayed was the beloved people whom God had committed to his care: "May God bless the First Presbyterian Church! Amen."

He was deeply interested in the children and youth of his congregation, and spoke of them during the last hours of his life with the utmost affection. He deeply regretted that he had not been able to be oftener among the children, and said that their teachers had claimed his particular anxiety. "Many of them," said he, "are Christians, and are undoubtedly prepared to teach the way of salvation to others; but many are strangers to the covenants of promise and know not Christ themselves, and are therefore unable to teach those under their care." He further said: "The young ladies and gentlemen of the church have always been a source of solicitude to me. There are many who have embraced Jesus Christ and are giving evidence of a Christian life, but some, I am fearful, have forgotten God. Those who are yet strangers to grace have had my prayers, and I humbly hope they may embrace the Saviour."

But his thoughts were not confined to the people of his charge. A few days before his death by a friend he sent the following message to his presbytery: "Tell my brethren in the ministry that this is the testimony of twenty-five years' service. My foundation of faith standeth sure, rest-ing in Jesus Christ. Though I have many imperfections—and no one knows them better than myself—yet his blood has blotted them all out. I approach him not in my own righteousness—that would not stand a single glance of his eye—but in his spotless righteousness."

His interviews with his family were especially touching. A few days before his death he called them around his bed, and after addressing himself to each one, he requested them to sing a part of that sweet hymn which has been such a solace to many pious hearts:

"Just as I am, without one plea,
But that thy blood was shed for me,
And that thou bid'st me come to thee,
O Lamb of God, I come, I come.
Happy day, happy day!
Here in thy courts we'll gladly stay,
And at thy footstool humbly pray
That thou would'st take our sins away!"

Of his personal views and feelings he spoke with the utmost confidence: "I wish it understood, that in view of the testimony I have borne in the pulpit and otherwise on the subject of religion, and on the doctrines of the Bible, I would change nothing. My views are the same as heretofore." As to his personal acceptance in Christ, he said, "I have not a shadow of doubt. The great source of my comfort and joy is in the full and free promises of God." Contemplating his departure, he said:

"Sweet to rejoice in lively hope
That when my change shall come,

Angels shall hover round my bed,
And waft my spirit home."

And again:

"Jesus can make a dying bed
Feel soft as downy pillows are,
While on his breast I lean my head,
And breathe my life out sweetly there."

His courage, faith and hope rose as his bodily powers failed; and but a short time before the spark of life was extinguished, upon being handed a glass of water from his own well—water for which he had a special fondness—he remarked, "I think it will not be long now till I taste the water of the Great Fountain and never thirst again. Oh for that one draught! that would be enough! Come, Lord Jesus, come quickly! Why, oh why, do thy chariot wheels delay? I long to depart and be with Christ!" And then, feeling that his time had come, and that, indeed, "angels were hovering round his bed to waft his spirit home," he seemed fully to realize that his last enemy was overcome, and he exclaimed, "*The battle's fought, the victory's won.*" Fitting words with which to close an honoured and useful life! But it must not be supposed he was exulting in his own strength—that he was assuming any honour to himself, or claiming that anything had been effected by his unaided power. No, he would have been the first to say, in his own calm, clear, earnest way, "It is all of grace." He was a victor by the grace of God. Every enemy was conquered—even the last, which is death; and as he saw them prostrate at his feet, with his very last breath he shouted *victory!* but had he been able to add more, it would have been, "Not unto me, O Lord, not unto me, but unto thy name give glory, for thy mercy and for thy truth's sake."

> "That man lives greatly,
> Whate'er his fate or fame, who greatly dies,
> High flushed with hope, where heroes shall despair."

Thus passed from among us, in the prime of his days, on the 26th of September, 1867, this faithful and accomplished minister of Jesus Christ. "It is the Lord's doing; it is marvellous in our eyes." But, conscious that God is infinitely wise and good, and that he knows far better than we what is best, both for his servants and his Church, we bow to his holy will and say, with the smitten patriarch, "The Lord gave and the Lord hath taken away; blessed be the name of the Lord!"

THE PROPHET ELISHA.

CHAPTER I.

THE CALL OF ELISHA.

THE first mention we have of the prophet Elisha occurs in the divine direction given to Elijah for his anointing in the elder prophet's stead. This command implied important purposes on the part of Jehovah, that were directly adapted to encourage his servant in a time of overwhelming dejection. Elijah was a man of bold and energetic decisions, but just such men as he are quite prone to indulge sanguine expectations at one time, and at another to fall into the opposite extreme of an unreasonable despondency. We admire the courage of this prophet when he dared to rebuke the guilt of Israel's perverse king; when he challenged the priests of Baal to a public controversy; when he dared to carry out the divine law by shedding the blood of the vanquished idolaters at the foot of Mount Carmel. Yet we wonder that so bold a man quails so easily at the threat of an imperious woman. It seems a strange inconsistency that he so quickly betakes himself to flight and strives so hard to save his life, while so lately he voluntarily put that life in peril, and indeed now querulously wishes it were taken away from him. The truth is, Elijah was a disappointed man—disappointed as a servant, who had zealously and faithfully attempted to do his Lord's will; the high expectations he had formed of usefulness had suddenly been dashed down. But he was disappointed according to the usual disappointment of pious men, not because their Lord is unfaithful, but because they themselves are foolish, self-willed, shortsighted. When the onward progress of Elijah's success took a sudden and apparently a disastrous turn, he rashly concluded that all his efforts had been in vain. He had supposed that his great victory at Carmel would put down at once all opposition to the cause of true religion, would cause a reaction throughout all Israel in favour of their forsaken duties, and would revive everywhere the neglected worship of Jehovah's altars. But the fierce message of Jezebel seemed to blight all those fair anticipations, and the sanguine prophet sank into the depths of a despondency as inconsistent as it was unbelieving.

Here are valuable teachings for all later times, for not only are we here reminded that the most eminent of the ancient prophets were still men of like passions with ourselves (James v. 17), but we have evidences as excellent that the divine mercy forsakes not even his erring servant, and that God condescends to meet them on the low ground of their infirmities. Though Elijah fled for his life without the divine direction, he did not go without the divine care; and though, at the end of his journey, the reproving voice asked, "What dost thou here, Elijah?" yet, through angelic ministry and with particular kindness, strength for that very journey had been specially afforded. The people of God may often recognize a divine, and indeed a special, care over them wherever they go, without being justified in arguing from this the divine approval of their thoughts and conduct. Even when Elijah was fed by an angel, he was a wandering prophet, and the extraordinary presence of his God upon Horeb is to inquire what call of duty had brought him there. God forsakes not, though man is ignorant, self-willed, easily dejected, ready to form rash conclusions.

Elijah, in this desponding hour, made many mistakes. He was mistaken in estimating his own usefulness, and in thinking that his labours were thus far in vain. He was mistaken in supposing that he alone was faithful among the tribes of Israel. He was mistaken in judging that the work to which he had devoted his life could be completed as rapidly as he had recently hoped, or arrested as easily as he had more lately feared. The divine voice, directly or indirectly, corrects all these mistakes. Instead of his standing alone in all Israel, he is directly assured that there were seven thousand men who sympathized with him. These were not indeed of bold and open adherents to Jehovah, otherwise the prophet could not have been ignorant of them. Yet were they acceptable before God, since they had not fallen in with the dominant idolatry. He was mistaken in supposing that Jezebel could put a speedy end to his reforming labours. Such great things in the orderings of God's providence usually proceed quite too slowly for man's impatience; they are less advanced by signal successes and less hindered by disheartening reverses than man is prone to judge; and they may be expected to go forward through more than the lifetime of any single person. God's hand might be in the prophet's labours, notwithstanding the sudden disastrous change that has disappointed Elijah; and he is indirectly taught this by being told that the work shall go on by those who shall be successors to Ahab and Jezebel and Elijah. The token is, that Elijah must anoint successors for himself in the prophetical office, and for the rival monarchs of Israel and Syria in the kingly. God's work must go on after Ahab has ceased to withstand it, after Elijah has ceased to promote it. This is the divine answer to human despondency. The Church of God is not arrested for every bold attack of blustering foes. Let disappointed believers in every age put away their dejection by taking larger views of the divine working. God's purposes fail not, though man mistakes their interpretation. Many friends and foes of Zion shall pass away, while, through many changes, God's great plans move on.

And when Elijah was thus directed to call Elisha to the prophetical office, he was himself not only encouraged by learning that his work was still to go on, but he was directed into a new and important channel of usefulness. When the prophet in his folly wished to die, God, who had provided better things for him, made no answer to this request—took indeed no notice of it—but turned his thoughts away to pressing engagements. That the work of Elijah must go on after he has left the earth is assurance that Ahab and Jezebel cannot stop it. That Elisha is to be anointed includes a new work of prophetical instruction, by the doing of which Elijah shall be speedily lifted from his present dejection. Believers have oftentimes no means of escape from dejecting fears but in putting forth energetic activities. The mind, doing nothing abroad, eats in upon itself, like rusting iron; while, according to the proverb, "The used key is always bright." Providence, by its manifest orderings, may lay a man aside from active duties. In that case he may be happy and cheerful while suffering the will of God. But when a man is idle through indolence or unbelief or dejection, though the path of active duty lies open before him, it is no wonder if he falls into discouragement and even despondency. This is the true solution of many complaints in the Church of God. Afflicted Christians are often happy; a sick and dying chamber is often a scene of triumph; an imprisoned apostle, who would gladly drop his chains to wear himself out in preaching, can yet joyfully say, God is doing good by my bonds. But inactivity must not be self-imposed. Indolent professors of the name of Christ give very poor evidences of piety, enjoy few comforts of religion, and may go halting and complaining until they arouse to their urgent active duties. They who would enjoy the bread of our Father's house must do the Father's will. "If any man do not work, neither shall he eat." Elijah was happy and the ravens fed him when the Lord had bidden him sit down by the brook Cherith, Elijah complains and wishes to die when, under the impulses of his own despondency, he forsakes his work and wanders off to the wilderness.

The direction to anoint Elisha as his successor reminds us that the call to the prophetical office in the ancient dispensation of the Church was special and extraordinary. There were teachers in that age who did not possess prophetical gifts in the higher sense; these were, sometimes at least, called the sons of the prophets; and from these, as we judge, men are divinely chosen oftentimes for the more complete discharge of these great duties. We have no instance of the exercise of the prophetical office except by the divine designation of the person. But a divine call does not supersede the propriety of instruction under competent teachers. That Elijah is to anoint Elisha—that the prophetic spirit is to rest largely upon him—opens a new sphere of duty, for Elisha became the pupil of Elijah; perhaps ten years were spent by these men conjointly, and at the end of this period they were separated. We do not judge that Elisha was nothing but a pupil all this time. But when Elijah began to teach, he taught others besides Elisha; after a little time the younger prophet was associated with him in these labours; indeed other associates were also found. They seem to have established schools of the prophets at various places; at Bethel, at Jericho, it may be at Samaria; by the labours of these men, scattered over the land as public teachers, the great reformation begun by Elijah was even more effectively and rapidly carried on after he was gone; so that at last the worship of Baal, against which Elijah fought, was entirely extirpated from Israel under Jehu and Elisha—that is, under the very king and prophet whom God bade his desponding servant anoint.

There is no better way to bless a land than to raise up for it religious teachers. We can scarcely attach too great importance to the liberal establishment of those higher schools of learning by whose efficiency young men are trained for the ministry of the Church. The best prophets of the Church—Samuel, Elijah, especially our Lord himself—spent their best energies in training men who should go forth as public teachers. A chief influence of our Lord's own ministry was in this remarkable thing, that in the three years of his public life he taught and sent forth more than fourscore preachers.

The call of Elisha was apparently unexpected to him. In this matter God deals with different men in different ways. A man may be consecrated by a mother's piety, and so trained that all Israel may know from his childhood that the godly Samuel is to be a prophet of the Lord; or he may be suddenly changed from a persecutor to a preacher, and as unexpectedly sent "far hence to the Gentiles." We have no information of Elisha's early life, no insight into his spiritual history, no record that he was called first to the faith and then to the ministry. Yet his introduction is less abrupt than that of Elijah himself, of whom we know nothing in the sacred history until we hear of his denunciation of wrath upon sinning Israel. We suppose that Elisha was now in early life. He was old enough to have the charge of his father's servants in the labours of the field, yet he was young enough to exercise his ministry for a length of time exceeded by only a few of the ancient prophets. Samuel, called in his childhood, lived perhaps over a hundred years; Isaiah lived in four, perhaps in five, reigns; Daniel lived during the entire period of the Babylonish captivity; Elisha lived in the reigns of six kings. He was called perhaps as much as ten years before the death of Ahab; the four succeeding kings whom he survived reigned fifty-nine years; and he probably died in the fifth year of the reign of Joash. We may well consider that as an important ministry which holds a position of great influence in Israel during a period of seventy or seventy-five years and in eventful times.

Elijah passed by and laid his mantle upon the young man's shoulders. Doubtless the coming of the prophet awakened his respectful attention, but this unexpected call stirred the very depths of his soul. He is ready to go when called to such a service, and yet he goes not thoughtlessly. He gives a token that he knows somewhat of the path in which he is beckoned forward, and that he feels the responsibility he so cheerfully assumes. And the elder prophet wishes him to understand and weigh the responsibility, as his act and speech would indicate. We need not suppose indeed that Elijah said no more to him than is here recorded, but all he said is consistent with the brief record here made. He significantly cast his mantle upon him. When Elisha signified his readiness to accompany him as his disciple—perhaps looking further to the prophetic office—and simply desires, through natural affection, to bid farewell to his parents, the words of Elijah are designed, possibly, to test his thoughts. As Naomi bade Ruth return to her kindred, though she was glad of her company, so Elijah bade this young man go back again, to know what was in his heart. We are not told that Elisha did go to kiss his father and his mother, but he tarried long enough to offer sacrifices to God, which betoken his serious sense of those new engagements, and his anxious desire to secure the blessing of Jehovah upon them.

Thus beginning his new course of lifelong duties, it may properly be thought that Elisha understood how serious were his new engagements. The ministry he now began was undertaken in no ordinary times, and we may well anticipate an energetic service from one who was willing to follow Elijah then. This young man was not ignorant of the bold stand which the prophet had taken a few weeks before, nor of the threats which Jezebel had uttered, nor of the self-denials and perils to which a companion of the Tishbite must be exposed. There was as much true courage in beginning a prophet's studies at such a time as this as in withstanding the gathered idolaters at Carmel. But they who go at the Lord's bidding, go under the Lord's protection; and ease, peace, and even personal safety, may be cheerfully surrendered by those who have divine promises of returns an hundred-fold.

CHAPTER II.

ELIJAH AND ELISHA.

ELIJAH and Elisha, associated together for so many years and uniting their influence for present and future good in Israel, were men of widely different characters. God employs various servants for his great work, and it is an important matter that we should wisely consider the diversities of his prophets. We see diversity as great in our own day in the ministry of the gospel. Let us not speak of the differences which spring from man's folly and ignorance and sin. Doubtless many preachers of the word would be more acceptable and useful toward man, and would bring more honor to religion and to God, if they were more prayerful, serious and diligent to learn and do the duties of the sacred office. But at the best, infirm men minister in holy things; and this is divinely allowed for many reasons—because they minister to imperfect people, and speak to their necessities, since they themselves "are compassed with infirmity;" because the mutual sympathies of minister and people have much to do for the ends of the ministry; because, especially, the feebleness of the instruments used magnifies that divine efficacy which wins the souls of men, "we have this treasure in earthen vessels." So long as any ministry is sincere and truthful, let no man despise its feebleness nor scorn an humble sermon, for God may magnify thus the excellency of his power.

But it is divinely appointed that the ablest earthly ministries are wonderfully different. One man is a "son of thunder;" another, a "son of consolation;" one is better suited to awaken careless consciences; another to direct inquiring penitents; another to instruct the people of God. Eminent men are rare in the ministry; as indeed they are in all the walks of life. One Paul, one Demosthenes, one Newton may be found in the lapse of ages; the mass of men learn piety and philosophy from ordinary teachers. The various gifts of men may be profitably employed with all their differences. The same tune may be played upon an organ or upon a flute; both may be melodious, yet are they not alike. Men are wise when they listen to the voice of the gospel, no matter by what lips or in what tones it is proclaimed in their ears. Still is it the grand old tune—

"Salvation, oh the joyful sound!"

Our Lord censures the men of his age because they found fault with John the Baptist and himself, and found excuses for listening to neither. One mingled too much with the people; the other, too little; one was too austere, the other too free. "But wisdom is justified of her children."

These two great prophets of the ancient Church were very different men. They belonged to the same general period: the younger loved the elder, as a son loves his father; they laboured together and aimed at the same great results, but they differed from each other, as God's ministers often differ, who occupy successively the same field of labor, and who are often providentally fitted for co-operating influences only the better because they are not alike.

It is not needful, perhaps not possible, and indeed it may not be desirable, to decide which was the prophet of superior influence. The remarkable close of Elijah's career seems to give token of his superior acceptance before God. Yet this may be less so than our first thought would judge.

One of the most interesting and instructive lectures I have read from the English preacher, Melville, is an elaborate effort to show that a larger interest and usefulness gathers about the feeble deathbed of the aged Elisha than belongs to the splendid ascension of Elijah in the chariots of Israel.

These prophets belong to an age of miracles. Two things may attract our wonder in the sacred Scriptures respecting miracles: *First*, That these writings are attested to men by plain and abundant miracles; and *second*, That the absence of miraculous powers is as remarkable during most of the scriptural history as their presence at others. A boasted advocate of the Romish Church in modern days has ventured the assertion that the whole history of God's people, from the beginning of the world down to the time of our blessed Saviour, was nearly a continued series of miracles.* The error of this statement is nearly as gross as the affirmation he appends, that the Church of Rome attests her divine origin by a continual appeal to miracles yet wrought by her teachers. Only a Church that neglects the study of the Bible could make the blunder of declaring that miracles are a standing mark of the true Church. Rather, according to the teachings of the Scriptures, the power to work miracles has belonged to very few prophets from the beginning until the time of Christ, and this is but an occasional and not a permanent mark of the Church.

There are two classes of scriptural miracles that may be conceived of as entirely distinct:

1st. Those wrought directly by divine agency, with little human instrumentality intervening, or none at all.

2d. Those wrought by the hands of God's servants, and eminently by his incarnate Son, who have thus given irrefragable proof of their divine commission.

To the first class belong such wonders as the Confusion of Tongues, the Flood, the Destruction

* Milner's End of Controversy, Letter xxiii.

of Sodom in the earlier records; the wonders wrought in Babylon as recorded in the book of Daniel in later times, together with wonders announced, in judgment or mercy, by the prophets at various times, which are clearly distinct from the exercise of miraculous powers of the second class we name. (See 1 Sam. vii. 10; xii. 18; 2 Sam. xxiv. 13; 2 Kings xix. 35; xx. 10.)

To the second class appertain three cycles of miracles. The most illustrious and the longest continued of these was connected with the ministry of God's own incarnate Son. When Christ came, as was fitting, miracles were abundantly wrought by him and his apostles to prove so great a thing as the advent of man's Redeemer. So far from continual miracles before that great period, only *four* men and only *two* periods in all the world's history were distinguished by these marvellous proofs of God's working by them. In one period, Moses and his successor Joshua; in another, Elijah and his successor Elisha wrought these wonders. We have no record that Abraham, Samuel, David, Isaiah or Daniel ever wrought miracles, though they witnessed wonders wrought directly by divine power. The especial reason for the exercise of these remarkable powers by Moses, and pre-eminently by our Lord Jesus Christ, lay in the propriety of authenticating their divine commission. Moses was in a very high sense a revealer of the divine will and the first of inspired writers. Christ Jesus made still higher claims and supported them by proofs the most illustrious. The reformation wrought in Israel in the days of Elijah and Elisha may rank in higher importance, because it was marked by the exercise of these extraordinary powers.

These two prophets were both workers of miracles, yet as their characters, so their ministries and their miracles are widely different. As we look upon their miracles, those of Elijah are more stupendous, those of Elisha are more numerous. The elder prophet is bold and rational, the younger is milder and more domestic. The one addresses the entire people, sends the dismay of a three years' drought through all the land, boldly reproves the wickedness of monarchs, engages in public controversy with the whole body of the idolatrous priesthood, and vindicates human and divine law by their slaughter on that fearful day of Carmel. The other prophet comes into the families of the land, heals the dangerous spring and the poisoned pot; appreciates the hospitality of the Shunamite, and restores to life the child of his benefactress; pities the poverty of the prophet's widow; and if great men and kings appear before him it is not that he boldly approaches them, but rather that they seek him out for counsel and relief. It is not proper to leave the impression that these contrasts are completely characteristic and without any exceptions. Elijah did not wholly lack kindly sympathy and the domestic feeling. He dwelt in a widow's household, and he too raised to life the son of his benefactress. So Elisha had his public duties and public influence. Yet in general the comparison is just. Elisha mingled more with the social life of the people, was more easily approached by them when they needed sympathy, and found his usefulness in domestic scenes.

The miracles of Elisha are usually more beneficent than those of his predecessor. We stand in awe of the stern tones and fearful wonders of the Great Reformer. Doubtless the times needed such a man, and he was equal to their worst aspects. But to shut up the heavens for three long years, to settle his dispute with Baal's prophets by the stern arbitrament of the sword, and to call down fire from heaven to consume the insulting messengers of King Ahaziah, are the awe-inspiring tragedies of Elijah's history. Even Elisha begins his separate ministry by the sternest scene of all his life; and, not without good reason, brings a judgment not easily forgotten upon the mocking youth of Bethel. Except this and Gehazi's leprosy, the wonders recorded of this prophet are remarkable for kindness and benevolence. He raised the dead, cleansed the leprous, fed the hungry with means that seemed quite inadequate, and relieved the poor; while scarcely a harsh word escaped his lips and scarcely a deed of severity marked his life.

We have suggested that the miraculous period to

which these prophets belonged is intermediate between two other periods—of Moses and of Christ. We may further notice that the miracles of Elijah, who stands nearer to Moses, are more like those of Moses; and the miracles of Elisha, who of the two stands nearer to Christ, are more like those of Christ. The same striking difference exists between Moses and Christ that also exists between Elijah and Elisha. The superior benevolence of our Lord's miracles over those of Moses any one may see. Christ upon one occasion refused to imitate one of Elijah's miracles, and gave this significant reason, "The Son of man is not come to destroy men's lives, but to save them," Luke ix. 56. Moses was a prophet of the law and its judgments. He scourged guilty Egypt with terrible plagues, and at last drowned their hosts in the Red Sea. But the great Author of the gospel came upon a different errand, and he marked his life by wonders which in every instance were benevolent.

Now as Moses and Elijah seem to bear like characters, so the character of Elisha seems similar to that of Christ. It was even his peculiar privilege to anticipate and foreshadow the workings of our blessed Lord; so that, though Christ Jesus, as becomes the Son of God, has a signal pre-eminence over all the servants in the Lord's house, we can scarcely read the miracles of Elisha without being reminded of those of Christ. Especially the healing of Naaman's leprosy, the restoring of a dead body to life and the feeding of a hundred men with a few loaves, are miracles, like in kind, though of inferior magnitude, to Christ's healing lepers by a word, raising the dead body of Lazarus and feeding thousands with a few barley loaves. And none but Elisha ever did anticipate, even in feeble measure, the gracious workings of Christ.

And not only the works, but the spirit also, of Elisha is more Christ-like. We find no fault with the prevailing spirit of the respective ministries of Moses and Elijah in the sphere assigned to each by divine providence. Various as are the works and ways of God, they are not clashing. In the economy of nature the thunderstorm that awes us by the fierce warring of the elements is as needful in its time as the bright shining of the vernal sun or the mild breathing of the evening zephyr. In the moral world man needs the fire, the storm and the earthquake, as well as the still small voice. This is a world of sin, and we cannot dispense with the awe-inspiring terrors of God's violated law. We recognize the truth and righteousness of that law whose ministers these elder prophets were. Neither does Christ make war against Moses, nor Elisha against Elijah, though between them the differences are so marked. Those who preach the law with all its terrors serve in the same ministry with those who commend the gospel in all its grace. Moses was faithful in all his house as a servant; the close of Elijah's ministry sufficiently attests his acceptable service. But the ministry of Elisha was milder. To him might be applied Isaiah's language, anticipating the ministry of the Messiah: "He shall not strive nor cry; neither shall any man hear his voice in the streets."

Perhaps the ministry of Elisha was needed to supplement that of Elijah, and the success of the truth among the Israelites of their age was due to their joint labours. Our Lord sent forth his disciples two by two; it has often been noticed that two men of dissimilar characters, exercising their ministry together among the same people or succeeding each other, find increased usefulness from their very diversities. In such cases the bold naturally comes first. The stern, energetic Luther needs the mild and scholarly Melancthon; the bold Elijah is aided by the gentle, laborious Elisha; even our Lord had a forerunner, who came in the spirit and power of an Elijah. Elijah's labours were but preparatory. He was like John the Baptist; he called men to repentance; he bade them "flee from the wrath to come." But alarming preaching, however needful, is not complete. The souls of men need what our elder divines would call *a law ministry;* but the law works wrath, and in its best offices but leads to Christ. Perhaps this was the divine lesson taught to Elijah in that great vision of the storm, the earthquake and the fire, and the Lord not in either of them. Elijah was like the ploughman who is needed to break up the ground, but the casting in of the seed is a quieter work which must needs precede the harvest. And Elijah learned the lesson. Associating with himself the son of Shaphat, they bent their joint efforts for ten years to the quiet duty of raising up religious teachers; they touched the hearts of the people by the still small voice of instruction, and precious results were soon visible. The ground had been thoroughly broken, and now the seed grew rapidly. When Elijah fled to Horeb, so few effects of his law ministry were visible that he complained that he stood alone; yet from the call of Elisha and their joint ministry we read of no more persecutions; the people seem to have gradually returned to the worship of Jehovah, notwithstanding the unfriendly influence of Ahab and Jezebel; and only two years after Elijah's ascension the new king, Jehu, by one single stroke, utterly blotted out Baal-worship from the kingdom of Israel for ever.

As the highest model of the ministry is found in our Lord Jesus Christ, we may justify the doctrines and influence which God honours in any man, but we may rather admire those who are most like the great Master. This honour belongs in no ordinary degree to the prophet Elisha: his history may enforce to us many a precious lesson of the gospel of Christ; and our interest should be the greater as we learn that the old and new in the Church of God affirm the same law and testify to the same grace.

CHAPTER III.

THE TRANSLATION OF ELIJAH.

A PERIOD of perhaps ten years intervened from the first call of Elisha until the translation of Elijah. Encouraged by the assurance that there was so large a number of faithful men in Israel by the direction to anoint successors for the kingly and prophetical offices, and especially by the divine declaration that Elisha should live to complete the reformation from Baal-worship, now happily begun in the land; instructed doubtless by the great vision on the holy mount, and cured for the rest of his life of his tendencies to despondency in the Lord's work, Elijah returned from the wilderness, called Elisha to share his labours, and spent his remaining years in new and more quiet forms of service. There were indeed public acts in the life of Elijah which belong to a later period than his association with Elisha, but they confirm the idea that a great change was secured by the controversy at Carmel. With all her fierceness of tone, Jezebel did not venture to carry her threats into execution. From this time forward, persecution of the prophets ceased and quiet reigned in

Israel. The royal family was not reformed, but it was awed. The seizure of Naboth's vineyard shows, on the one hand, how an humble man dared to stand up for his rights even against the court, though, on the other hand, it exhibits the cunning of the unscrupulous queen to effect her wicked end. Arbitrary power dared not openly show itself, as heretofore; the laws of the kingdom were sustained by public opinion, as they were not in the earlier years of Ahab; even the king must cover up his violence under the form of legal proceedings; and Jezebel would not resent the prophet's bold and open reproof which denounced her own and Ahab's death for their iniquity against Naboth. The controversy on Carmel was not in vain. Elijah had fled from the land, driven by false fears. The people felt as they had not before; with all her malice, Jezebel would not have dared to execute her threat: perhaps the very warning given to the prophet was proof of her weakness; Elijah was safe on his return, as he would have been safe if he had not fled at all.

Under these favourable changes in public opinion the two prophets began their joint ministry. A few years after this, Ahab died by wounds received in battle, and the dogs of Samaria licked his blood, according to Elijah's word. Meanwhile the prophets were doing a needful work. God forsook not Israel. In his great love to a degenerate people, more excellent prophets were given in this age to

Israel than to Judah, because they were more needed; and the pious portion of the people required special support (Patrick). We will not attempt, however, to describe the humble labours of which so little is said. It often happens that the most valuable work done for the good of any community attracts but little notice and receives but brief record. Like the foundation of a magnificent building, which is costly, but not sightly, and which indeed is hidden under the ground, while it supports the whole of what is visible, the labours of teaching are modest, little appreciated and little spoken of; but they are truly the foundation upon which individual and national greatness must hereafter rest.

But the time came when these two prophets were no longer to be associated. Elijah in his petulance had wished to die prematurely; God dealt with him better than this; the prophet was not to die at all. Almost alone of all the human race, it was the privilege of this holy prophet to leave the earth in an extraordinary manner, without the pangs of dying.

> "The second man that leaped the ditch
> Where all the rest of mankind fell,
> And went not downward to the sky."

We are not told how much anticipation Elijah had of this wonderful event, but it seems evident from the narrative that it was separately revealed to both the prophets, and either gathered from their serious demeanour, or learned also from on high, by their disciples. What seems strange is, that the elder prophet seems unconscious of the penetration of the younger, and disposed to separate from his company, that he may meet this great change alone. But Elisha, fully aware that their parting hour drew near, though perhaps having as yet no understanding of the method by which it should be effected, desirous of prolonging their intercourse while he may, and anxious to render any service which might possibly belong to the mysterious event before them, refused to be left behind on any pretext whatever. So they journeyed both together, and this perhaps for several days before the final parting. Elijah was desirous of visiting the various schools of the prophets, and of addressing to them his last counsels, yet without the formal announcement that they should see his face no more. Even between the two, the deep consciousness that these are their last days of earthly friendship seems to have found no expression in words.

The elder prophet has lost none of his interest in his earthly work because it is so nearly done and heaven is just before him. This is one of the excellences of religious services, that our work gives more abundant satisfaction as we draw near the confines of eternity—our interest in it abides and follows us beyond the grave. How gladly would we listen while Elijah and Elisha talk of their great duties so near to their parting! Yet how singular to notice that they keep down all allusions to the event so close at hand, at least until just before the grand conclusion! This may have been from that natural feeling which we so often find it hard to break over—that in ordinary life makes us shut our eyes to our evidently approaching separations. Our brethren languish before our eyes; dangerous symptoms warn us, fearful forebodings depress us: friends tell us, "Know ye not that the Lord is about to take away;" yet we refuse to realize the unwelcome teaching; we bid them hold their peace, as we hold our own, and we are surprised at last by the unexpected close at which no one else is surprised. Yet the prophets are more communicative when Elijah knows that Elisha will not leave him. We may properly believe that they spent their final hours in closing counsels, to be recalled and valued by Elisha for many days afterward.

As they passed on, the tokens of the great event became more manifest. Leaving Jericho, they approached the Jordan. In the ordinary language of our religious life, we are so accustomed to speak figuratively of the river Jordan, that divided the wilderness where Israel so long wandered from the Canaan of their promised rest, to make it significant of death itself, that like a narrow river separates our earthly trials and duties from our immortal life, that we see a great propriety in

Elijah's last miracle. He who is about to be translated that he may not see death may well cleave the Jordan and pass through dry-shod. And having thus signified to Elisha what is so soon to happen, he throws off his reserve, speaks directly of being taken from him, and gives him the opportunity of asking what he will before their parting. And Elisha asked, what even Elijah esteems a hard thing: "And Elisha said, I pray thee let a double portion of thy spirit be upon me." Commentators differ as to the meaning of the request. They judge it lacks modesty to ask for twice as large a portion as Elijah had: they usually prefer to understand the double portion as a reference to the privilege allotted to the first-born son, to whom was given eminence over his brethren, and, as a token of it, a double portion of the father's estate. See Deut. xxi. 17. So Jacob took away Reuben's birth-right for his misconduct, and gave Joseph a portion above his brethren, Gen. xlviii. 22. "So the birth-right was Joseph's," 1 Chron. i. 2. They therefore judge that among the sons of the prophets Elisha desires to be declared the successor of Elijah. But it is inconceivable that of such a request Elijah would say, "Thou hast asked a hard thing." For Elisha seems to have been designated for his successor; and God's positive direction for his anointing was given respecting none other, and the assurance was added that he should complete Elijah's work. "Elisha shalt thou anoint to be prophet in thy room," and "him that escapeth from the sword of Jehu shall Elisha slay," 1 Kings xix. 17, are words that sufficiently designate his succeeding to Elijah's work.

Perhaps we may get a better and simpler understanding of this request by remembering that Elijah's prophetic spirit was itself a twofold portion above God's ordinary prophets; and this Elisha desires to secure. We have already noticed that the power of working miracles was uncommon in the Church. Up to this period of the world's history before Elijah, only Moses and Joshua had possessed the rare faculty. Eminent prophets had spoken in the name of God, but had wrought no miracles. This was an extraordinary combination of spiritual gifts. Elijah had it; would it be given or withheld from his successor? This was a question too hard for the prophet to answer. He must refer it directly to God; all he can do is to suggest the token of a favourable answer. And Elisha said, "Let, I pray thee, the portion of double, which has been on thy spirit, be also upon me." He desired the elder prophet's DOUBLE-PORTIONED GIFTS. He had asked what Elijah thought a great thing; but that God who is never offended by his people's large requests was pleased to answer. He did see the elder prophet as he was taken from him; moreover he did possess this twofold honour, and wrought miracles more abundantly than did Elijah; and it seems to have been at the sight of his first miracle that the sons of the prophet recognized in him all he had thus asked. They easily discerned that he no longer possessed simply the ordinary powers of a prophet, but the extraordinary qualifications of Elijah. They saw the parted waters of the Jordan, and said, "The spirit of Elijah does rest on Elisha."

After the request was made, the two walked and talked together, and soon after were suddenly separated. A chariot of fire and horses of fire appeared; Elijah was borne aloft; Elisha was left alone. Yet it was a great privilege that he saw the ascension. It was a sight never to be forgotten; often recounted perhaps in the ears of his people; often recalled to furnish glorious hopes of immortality; and the expression he used in parting with Elijah was to be repeated by bereaved friends long afterward at his own lamented departure. Why others of the people or the sons of the prophets were not allowed to witness this scene, we do not know. Some suppose that the sons of the prophets saw the translation across the Jordan. At least the apostles were allowed to see the simpler and more glorious ascension of Jesus. Doubtless the doctrines of the translation of Enoch and Elijah, in their respective ages, were explained and enforced in the hearing of their assemblies by their religious teachers, and the evidences and the consolations of piety were thereby increased. The august scene we vainly attempt to imagine. Elisha saw it. His prayer was granted. Not only so. In token that he needed earthly garments no more, and that Elisha was to possess all it signified, the ascending prophet dropped his mantle to the earth.

Elisha not only cried out, but gave also the usual Oriental sign of grief in that he rent his own clothes. It would seem to us surely that in this case, if in any departure from earth, there need be no lamentation, but Elisha might have been justified in a song of triumphal congratulation to the glorified prophet ascending thus in the chariots of Israel. But indeed here is substantially the same cause of sorrow that usually belongs to us when pious friends are removed. We mourn the righteous dead for our own sakes, not for theirs.

"When such friends part, 'tis the Saviour dies."

Even the translated Elijah is the lamented prophet. No matter how triumphant is the departure, the loss to the Church is the same; we are comforted concerning those that are prepared to go; and yet after all those who are most ready we may truly mourn, for we can little afford to lose them. Yet the very source of our sorrows in our loss should moderate our grief, especially when we reflect that the Lord God of Elijah removes his servant, and himself forsakes not his people.

So, as Elisha took up the prophet's mantle and turned his steps homeward, he gave proof of his faith in the pledge he had received by repeating

Elijah's wonder that he might recross the Jordan. He smote the river with the mantle, as he had seen Elijah do; he called upon the God of Elijah; the waters divided as before, and Elisha passed through. Both these miracles of the divided waters seem to have been witnessed by a company of the sons of the prophets to the number of fifty men, who had followed them as far as the river, but were not permitted to cross—who had wished to see the mysterious closing scene, but doubtless did not. As the time was short from Elisha's first crossing until his return alone, these men tarried still by the Jordan; and when they saw him repeat the wonder of Elijah, they readily recognized his right to wear the prophet's mantle and to take his place.

Yet these men could not realize the stupendous wonder that had taken place. Elijah had not died; he was still in the body; he was taken up by the winds; might he not be cast down again in some place where he might stand in need of their assistance. This expression seems to imply that the Spirit of God did sometimes miraculously transfer the prophets from one place to another. So when Obadiah was sent to tell Ahab, "Behold, Elijah is here," he feared that while he went the Spirit would bear the prophet away, 1 Kings xviii. 12. So the Spirit took up Ezekiel and transferred him to the children of the captivity, Ezek. iii. 12, 14; so the Spirit caught Philip away from the eunuch's chariot, Acts viii. 39. Indeed the question, What became of Elijah? has given great perplexity to the Jews in far later times; this none the less because of Malachi's prophecy that Elijah should come again. This we know our Lord interprets of John the Baptist, who came in the spirit and power of Elijah, Matt. xvii. 10–13; Luke i. 17. The sons of the prophets, in indefinite fears respecting him, requested permission to search for him. Elisha knew that all their searchings would be in vain, and refused to let them go. But upon their persistent importunity he granted permission. He was willing that they should be satisfied upon the subject; he would not seem wanting in any proper respect for Elijah; he would not assume authority too peremptory in such a case as this. But they thus learned their first lesson of Elisha's competency. As he said, so it proved. Their search was vain. Elijah was no more on earth, but had gone to the heavenly Paradise.

We may reasonably believe that the translation of Elijah was a great aid to the future influence of Elisha, so that it is impossible for us to judge of the usefulness of these two prophets as of two separate interests. There were not wanting some in that age that were skeptical and scoffing concerning the fact of Elijah's ascension—a skepticism which, as we shall see, laid the foundation of a divine rebuke which doubtless silenced all opposition in that matter. But we know that the enemies of good men often praise them after they are gone; and it would not be strange if they, the very opponents of Elijah, felt a new reverence for his counsels after he was taken away in a manner so remarkable. This event was designed to have its influence upon the welfare of the Church. Henceforward the friends of piety would find a large increase of faith and boldness, would rejoice in the divine consolations, would have higher anticipations of the future life. The ascension of Christ, we know, was the great joy and strength of his disciples. Elijah as a servant could not rise to the high measure of his Lord, yet it is reasonable to think that his translation was a glory and a power in that age to strengthen the hands of godly men and to confound the thoughts of opposers.

NOTE.—The mantle of Elijah is not once mentioned after the recrossing of the Jordan. No matter of what materials or shape, it is used in the inspired narrative as a symbol of Elijah's prophetic character; we need go no farther in our inquiries concerning it than to know this; and we have personally no sympathy with the affected discernment of that style of learning that finds in Elijah an exemplar of the Oriental dervish, or would speak of him as "the great Israelitish dervish." Smith's Dictionary, ii. 232; Stanley's E. Church, 443.

CHAPTER IV.

THE WATERS AT JERICHO HEALED.

THE first miracle recorded of Elisha was perhaps, as we have seen, in the sight of fifty men, the sons of the prophets. The new characteristic of his ministry, as foreshadowing the beneficent works of Christ, immediately appears. For the first time in the history of the Church, application was directly made to a prophet of God to do a beneficent miracle on behalf of the people. Moses brought water out of the rock to answer the murmurings of Israel; Elijah raised to life the widow's son when she, doubtless, looked for no such relief; but here the elders of the city, with a new sympathy toward a milder prophet, whom they may venture to approach, request Elisha to grant them a much-needed relief.

The city of Jericho had been destroyed by Joshua, and he had uttered a solemn curse against the man who should dare to rebuild it. This curse, in the days of Ahab, had fallen upon the family of Hiel, a man of Bethel, a city of whose wickedness we shall soon have further occasion to speak. Partaking of the unbelief of his people, he defied the warning of Joshua, and paid the penalty in the partial or entire destruction of his family. It may be that Joshua's curse was further fulfilled in the barrenness of the ground by reason of some peculiar quality of the water.

Modern travellers speak of a fine spring yet flowing near Jericho, which may be the one here spoken of. Dr. Thomson says: "In the afternoon we visited again Ain es Sultan" (*i. e.*, the Fountain of the Sultan; it is sometimes called the Fountain of Elisha). "This fountain rises at the base of a hill which has the appearance of an Indian mound, though rather too large for a work of art. But there are many similar *tells* in the plain, and they were probably thrown up for the same purpose as those which are so numerous in America. The water is sufficiently abundant to turn a large mill, is beautifully transparent, sweet and cool, and swarms with small fish. There seems to be no reason to doubt the tradition that this is the identical fountain whose bitter waters Elisha healed." * To this we add from Mr. Stephens that "several streams constantly running from it refresh and fertilize the plains of Jericho." †

It is made then an appropriate beginning of Elisha's ministry, since his prevailing spirit is evangelical, to remove the curse which had been pronounced by a sterner prophet; and the wonder

* The Land and the Book, ii. 449.

† Incidents of Travel, ii. 200.

becomes typical of Elisha's prophetic services. The city was pleasantly situated; but of what avail are other advantages if an element so important as water is wanting; or, worse than this, if unwholesome waters flow there? So may we judge in all moral matters. Here is a community having distinguished advantages of wealth and intelligence and freedom and influence; but what are all these if the waters of barrenness, unrighteousness and irreligion flow forth to curse the people? Here is a Church, possessing the Bible and the sanctuary and the ministry; but what are even these if the barren waters of formalism, falsehood and worldly conformity flow forth there? Here is an individual, who has his lot in a land of pleasantness and dwells in a goodly heritage; but he drinks not of the waters of salvation, and has not in him the grace of the Spirit springing up unto everlasting life. The design of the gospel is to heal the barren waters; its power alone can effect this. Let the salt of divine grace be cast into the springs of influence and the waters are changed. The pleasantness of the city becomes an abode, not cursed, but blessed of God. Elisha's miracle healed the waters by simple, apparently inappropriate means. He called for salt and a new cruse. All suspicion of any natural energy in the means employed is put away. He uses a new vessel, that the virtue may not be ascribed to something it had formerly contained; he uses salt, which is usually thought to induce rather than to cure sterility; so the power of healing is evidently from God, whose name he invokes. So Elisha's ministry is to be a blessing, and it has this appropriate beginning. From this miracle comes the familiar phraseology by which we speak of the salt of divine grace being cast into the sources of influence.

In his Synopsis, Matthew Pool quotes authorities for declaring that the Romish Church takes the practice of sprinkling holy water from this miracle of Elisha. "I wonder," he quaintly adds, "why it does not use figs, because Isaiah used them in healing Hezekiah's sore!" But Middleton proves that "holy water" has a pagan origin.

CHAPTER V.

THE JUDGMENT BY THE BEARS AT BETHEL.

WE may give a more careful consideration to the next miracle recorded of this prophet. Leaving Jericho, Elisha came to the city of Bethel. Here he was met by a crowd of rude boys, who mocked and jeered at him as he passed by the way. To understand this case, let us notice its several parts:

I. We are told there came forth "little children." But from the use of this term we are unable to decide much respecting the age of these persons. The same term is used in the Scriptures for persons who are doubtless far past the age of childhood. Isaac is termed a lad at a time when he was over thirty years old; and Solomon calls himself a "little child" when he was forty years of age, and actually king of Judah. See Gen. xxii. 12; 1 Kings iii. 7. So in various passages this word is used of adult persons, though not there usually with the word "little" (1 Sam. xxx. 17). The same may be said of a different word used in this narrative (in verse 24), which in 1 Kings xii. 8 is used for the young men, associates of King Rehoboam, he being then forty years old, who counselled him contrary to the advice of the old men. It is proper to judge that at least the ringleaders of this mob, upon whom fell the curse of the prophet, were of that larger class of riotous boys who are so often the pests of a disorderly town, whose reformation awakens the anxiety of our best citizens, and whose control demands the wisdom and energy of our best police.

II. This thing occurred at Bethel.

The name signifies "the house of God," and the early associations of the place are sufficiently delightful. There the weary patriarch Jacob laid him down to sleep, saw in a vision the angels of God ascending and descending, anointed his altar and bestowed the name—This is Bethel, the house of God, the gate of heaven! But, alas! times have changed in Bethel and with the descendants of Jacob! We may judge of the character of any people when we know what are their religious professions, and what are the institutions maintained and cherished among them. For eighty years past, Bethel had been one of the chief abodes of idolatry as practiced among the ten tribes of Israel. When Jeroboam became king of these tribes, he was afraid that his people, if allowed to go freely to worship at Jerusalem, might become reconciled to the family of David, and might overthrow the new kingdom. Accordingly, he wished to provide religious services at home. Himself corrupted with the idolatry of Egypt, where he had been long an exile (1 Kings xi. 40), he introduced the worship of two golden calves; erecting one at Bethel and the other at Dan, with the usual train of priests to maintain a magnificent style of worship. Thus he attempted to draw off the people from their allegiance to Jehovah. During the two or three generations that had passed away up to the times of Elisha, this corruption had full time to work; and we may easily judge that during the reign of Ahab the city of Bethel, as one of the chief seats of idolatry in the land, would be a warm partisan of Jezebel, and would be thoroughly hostile to the reforming efforts of Elijah.

It speaks well for the bold faithfulness of the Lord's prophets that they were ready to do their work even in the idolatrous city of Bethel. Elijah and Elisha established here one of the schools of the prophets. Thus they confronted idolatry in its very stronghold, and beyond question they used all their influence to bring the guilty inhabitants of the place to repentance. It is easy to understand that the power and influence of idolatry were greater in Bethel, because for the whole kingdom it was one of two great centres for that kind of worship, and doubtless of greater importance than the rival city of Dan. If Jeroboam had erected a golden calf in every town, then Bethel might have been no worse than neighbouring places. But the tribes all around them, in the most populous part of the kingdom, came to Bethel to worship; it was the Jerusalem of the Israelitish State, and the town owed its prominence, its worldly prosperity and its wealth to its golden god. Thus the Bethelites would naturally learn to glory in that worship which brought population and honour and wealth to their city; the golden calf which was their shame became their boast, and they could bear with nothing that in any wise reflected upon the rising institutions of idol-worship. People easily forget principles when their eyes are fixed on profits. The people of Bethel became deeply imbued with the abominable sentiments of Jeroboam and Jezebel; they taught their children to uphold the idol-worship, without which the flourishing city of Bethel would be reduced to a level with the insignificant towns around; and no small hostility was awakened against the school of the prophets, so opposed, as they would argue, to the true interests of the place. There would not be wanting men to stir up the baser passions of the people by reminding them that by this craft they had their wealth, and by the cry, "Great is the golden calf of Jeroboam!" The institution for training prophets to Jehovah was not popular at Bethel.

III. We may further notice the time and the significance of the insult offered to Elisha.

The time was upon his first appearing at Bethel after the ascension of Elijah. Some days certainly (2 Kings ii. 17, 18), or even some weeks, may have passed since that event; and the tidings had spread through Israel that the elder prophet had been taken up to heaven. Surely an event like this was adapted, if anything could be, to produce a deep impression upon all the people, and even to soften the hardened hearts of Elijah's most bitter enemies. When a good man is removed from the scenes of earth, it is a common thing for the voice of hatred and censure to die away; perhaps the respect due to his memory is called forth from lips that have reviled him; and indeed he may even receive loud praises from those who love his principles no better than before. That seems indeed a hatred more than usually bitter that survives the death of its object, and sends the shafts of calumny through the darkness that gathers over a grave. The ascension of Elijah was a departure from earth even more remarkable than death; and we would think that so signal a proof of the divine favour would secure, if nothing more, the silence of his foes. Such a life and such a departure! Could malice now say aught against these or him?

In Bethel, Elijah was well known. How were the tidings of his departure, in a manner so illustrious, received among that people? Perhaps with unbelief. Though they knew the proofs of divine power in him, and the sincerity and truthfulness of both the prophets, they may have ventured to attribute falsehood to Elisha when he proposed, with so bold a statement, to account for Elijah's disappearance.

But if even they disbelieved the translation, they doubtless believed that Elijah was no more on earth, and would appear no more among them. And these convictions filled Bethel with joy. This belief soon spread from one end of the city to the other; it was the theme on every lip, the topic of conversation in every household, that the chief teacher in that institution established to denounce the existing worship in Bethel was no more upon the earth. And now that Elijah was gone, they would gladly be rid also of Elisha. This perhaps was the sentiment of the city before they again saw Elisha. So, upon his first return to Bethel, they were prepared for his reception, and a rabble went forth to meet him, and to scoff at him in language personally insulting and jeeringly referring to the glorious ascension of Elijah. We need not judge that Elisha was really bald. He was scarcely old enough to lose his hair through age; and indeed in some Oriental countries this epithet is one of reproach applied to those that have plenty of hair. They meant it as a reproach, whatever may have been the prophet's personal appearance. But the chief insult was in the words, "Go up." It may have been the insulting language of unbelief. "Go up now: you tell us your master has gone up; let us have the proof of it in your own ascension before our eyes." It may express the bitter hatred the Bethelites bore toward these men of God; "Go up now; we are glad Elijah has gone; we will be glad also to be rid of you." Nor does there seem to be any possible interpretation that can be put upon the time, place, manner and terms of these insulting expressions toward this man of God that does not imply irreverence and hatred of all that is holy and excellent and venerable. A man of eminent purity of character is reviled; a prophet of exalted authority is insulted; the thing is done in the streets of a city where he spent at least a portion of his time, and had all the claims of a resident; and the basis of all unquestionably is, that the people were the degraded worshippers of Jeroboam's golden image, while this man was an honoured servant of the God of Israel.

In view of such thoughts it seems a matter of little importance to ask the age of the children who use language like this toward Jehovah's prophet. We gather from their conduct an estimate of the state of family training in that entire community; for if the household in Bethel had been respectful to these prophets, or had taught the reverence due from the people of Israel to the prophets of the God of Israël, no such mob, composed of children large enough to go out and meet Elisha, and to use such language toward him, could have been sent forth from the city. In any way we look fairly at the case, it is not hard to justify the prophet's curse. He turned back and cursed them in the name of the Lord. We must of course dismiss the thought of passion or profanity in such a man as he, and conceive of this thing as done with the utmost seriousness. He did this thing so by divine authority that his words fell not in vain. God answered the prophet's language by sending forth from the woods two fierce bears* which slew forty-two—perhaps the ringleaders of the crowd.

Now if we suppose that these were children of tender years we can justify this severity. For indeed nothing is more shocking to every proper feeling than to see irreverence and disrespect of serious things on the part of children. Let us not say that these are to be excused because of the immaturity of their faculties. Rather it is the mischievous and morbid maturity of principles that is exceedingly unnatural in a child. Youth is the period of simple and candid and respectful feelings; when children are found pert, forward, disposed to trample on the feelings or the rights of others, they have learned lessons already that belong not to their age; for when they are under a wise and wholesome discipline in the household, they pay a ready and cheerful homage to worth and piety. And what prospect was there that the boys of Bethel, who had already learned to mock at God's prophets and to ridicule so sacred a thing as Elijah's ascension, would become good and useful men in later years? If they were old enough to do this through their own malice and wickedness, they deserved the

* The Syrian bear is perhaps equally to be dreaded with the lion in a close encounter. The Land and the Book, i. 373.

judgment. If they were so young that their youth is any valid apology, then is the judgment and evidence of the divine displeasure upon their parents, without whose guilt no such scene could have occurred, and who were scourged in this fearful bereavement.

Taking the whole transaction as revealing the character of the population of that city, we may learn important lessons. The people of Bethel had gone far in apostasy from Jewish principles before such a scene of wickedness could take place there from any class of their children. No one thing is more characteristic of a true piety, according to the teachings of the sacred volume, than a profound impression of the importance and the responsibility of the parental office, as we are bidden to watch over, to rule and to train our children. But, alas! it is no peculiarity belonging to the ancient city of Bethel that a crowd of boys could be gathered upon the streets to mock at good things and to cast their ribald reproaches upon good men. There is scarcely perhaps a Christian city in this land, and in an age noted for its spreading light both of piety and civilization, where the like might not occur, and still cause but little surprise; and where, if such conduct did occur, there might not be found men to apologize for it on the score of the youthfulness of the offenders. As if, in view of the morals of the community, it did not rather make the matter worse to see depravity so ripe from seeds so lately sown! As if the promise of future mischief was not even more dreadful when children start so early on so bad a course! As if the vileness of the young was not the worst possible token of the state of religion and morals in the entire community! Why is it that men allow themselves to be so deceived as to wink at juvenile depravity, or to think that these things naturally tend to work their own cure? Has not experience always proved that evil habits grow stronger as the mind and body become mature? Sin gathers strength as the sinner grows older, and every evidence of youthful depravity is a dangerous forewarning of ripened iniquity in riper years.

Now we are taught by this judgment on the rabble at Bethel that God looks not lightly on these outbreakings of juvenile wickedness. The Scriptures wisely say: "Even a child is known by his doings," Prov. xx. 11. We may justly lay much of the responsibility upon the parent when we see early proofs of gross iniquity, but we are not to excuse either the parent or the child. Any man may, if he pleases, busy himself to define the exact limits of personal responsibility in each; it is not at all necessary for us to do anything of this kind; God has blended together the interests, duties and responsibilities of parents and children; and it is not possible, nor is it of any practical importance, to run the line between them. Our duties and responsibilities may be understood and enforced, though our social relations increase rather than lighten the burden. We are in no danger of putting too high an estimate upon a careful and religious training in early life; we should note here that God marks the iniquities of even youthful offenders; we should fear his judgments upon sinners, young or old, in Bethel or in any Christian city.

And indeed so long as man is the possessor of a depraved nature these salutary lessons cannot become obsolete, but retain their value for every age and community. Evils threatening the best interests of piety and the happiness of the young must be guarded against in each succeeding generation. There is perhaps a prevalent disposition for each age and each community to look back and complain of the decline of family order. How truly we might do this, let us not now inquire; doubtless many such comparisons are both incomplete and unwise. Eccles. vii. 10. But we can discern that in the families that usually fall under our notice, the training and discipline of the household are not as they should be; and if any other community is worse in these matters than we are, it but needs a deeper repentance, which yet lightens not at all the burden of our responsibilities. We may justly acknowledge that in the prospering communities of our Western States there is far more attention now given than could be given in the forming state of our society for the intellectual training of our children; while every true friend of education must acknowledge that much still remains to be done in regard to these important interests. But there are serious defects to be noticed and corrected in regard to the higher education of the heart and the conscience, and the preparation of the young for the direct service of their Creator. Take but this one suggestion. Nothing is easier to effect, if parents are but properly disposed to secure it—nothing would give better proof of a deep interest in the religious welfare of our families—few things are more important for their bearing upon the future than the attendance of our children upon the public services of religion. The attendance of children in any community upon the sanctuary and the Sabbath-school ought to be larger than that upon our public week-day schools. Many parents keep their children employed upon other days; but employments should be no interference upon Sabbath attendance. Yet our public schools are fully and punctually attended, as compared with the sanctuary and the Sabbath-school; and it is to be feared that those who most neglect these more public means of a religious education do but little for the pious training of their children in the household; and such contrasts are too good evidence of lamentable neglect of those high interests.

And the proofs lie not only in such negative considerations. We cannot shut our eyes from things that call forth a patriot's concern, a Christian's anxiety. In all our streets we may hear the vile utterances of profanity from boys, not even half grown; we may see their disgusting imitations of the vices of older ruffians, which not seldom require the interference of a police officer; we may witness the lounging and idleness, and even the boisterous rudeness, of Sabbath desecration upon the corners of our streets and around our suburbs; and we may listen to the weak excusings of parents, who apologize for their sinful neglect in the past and shameful inefficiency in the present in the confession, "We cannot control our children." These are matters of high concern. The evil is acknowledged. The divine judgment upon the juvenile profligates at Bethel may remind us that God overlooks not nor disregards the sins of youth. And knowing that evil things wax worse and worse, the whole matter needs thought and prayer and activity.

We cannot too thoroughly consider the dangers which beset the young, to lead them astray from the paths of piety and to bring upon them and us the just judgments of God. We should never overlook the serious truths that they are partakers of a sinful nature, that temptations attend every step of their going forward in life, and that there are no successful safeguards except those which prepare the heart itself to resist evil and to choose good. Wise restraints are valuable, but they are not enough. We must do more than keep from evil; we must train to holy thoughts and aims and deeds.

The basis of all is in the serious, prayerful, diligent contemplation of parental obligations. Can any responsibility be more serious than that which rests upon a parent? To him, in the early years of a child's immortal life, is committed a care so complete, so full of authority, so momentous, so controlling! Children are usually what their parents have made them. We cannot mean that the iniquity of youthful offenders is the designed result of parental training. This would be a wide misjudgment indeed. If only the children of profligate parents proved also profligate, the evils we deplore would be confined within narrower limits. The errors lie not so much in purpose as affection. Parents usually love their children, usually desire to see them become useful, honourable, upright men. There are other sources of difficulty.

The importance of forming only good habits of thought and word and deed in very early life is too little acknowledged; evil tendencies are undervalued; their dangerous nature is not perceived; it is thought they will exert no long influence; sometimes they are even applauded as proofs of intellect or spirit; and no careful energies are put forth to nip sin in the bud. Parents allow children to be in companies where they themselves would not go, and to do things which they would not do, as if there was less evil in exposure to temptation for a child than for an adult! Possibly, so far as present wrong is concerned, this judgment may be true; but so far as an influence for future mischief is concerned, it is certainly more dangerous to expose a child to temptation than an older person. The bad impression of one single misspent hour may never be effaced. Immature strength may be strained by a burden which a stronger muscle easily lifts. Many parents seem never to employ their common sense in the moral training of their children. They have an exquisite taste as to a daughter's dress, but the better part is neglected. A man who would not trust a bungling workman to make a coat or a boot, much less to build a house, yet judges that the reasonable and immortal beings whom God has committed to his care may be trained for this world and the next with no diligent and careful study and labour bestowed upon their moral culture. Ignorance and neglect on the part of parents do the young more mischief than even the busy tempters about them. Yet in such a case ignorance and neglect are inexcusable crimes, and their consequences are deplorably disastrous.

The rising generation are the hope of the Church and of the world, and Scripture and reason mark their youth as the golden season of improvement. Not peculiarly in religion, but in every sphere of life where lessons are to be learned, the young are apt pupils. While children are beneath the parental roof the character for life is usually formed. Youth may be the only time to teach our children, for they may soon be gone. If not the only time, it is still the best. Let us not judge that our children must first enjoy the world before they find their portion in God. So far as the world is innocent, they need not give it up for religion's sake; so far as the world is guilty, it is madness to make light of their attachment to it at any age. Nor should we judge that children are incapable of the knowledge and affections of true piety. In any school-room we may justly commend a child's improvement and intelligence, even though he belongs to the lowest class in the school, for we make allowances for what we should properly expect in each particular case. In a boy, as Legh Richmond properly says, we must look for "a boy's religion, a boy's knowledge, a boy's faith, and a boy's salvation;" and the Scriptures greatly encourage the approach of the young to their forgiving God.

Let the young draw near to God. They are specially invited. Well does Dr. Watts write—

> "'Twill save you from a thousand snares
> To mind religion young;
> Grace will preserve your following years,
> And make your virtues strong."

And God marks iniquity against the young. He said of the good young Josiah, "Because thine heart was tender, . . . I have heard thee," 2 Kings xxii. 19. But he saw and punished the scoffing youths of Bethel.

CHAPTER VI.

THE DISTRESSED ARMIES DELIVERED.

THE history of the prophet now becomes connected with the train of civil affairs in the kingdom of Israel. We read next of Elisha in the camp of war; and to understand the whole we must notice the ruling authorities in Israel, and the enemies and the allies of the kingdom.

Ahab was now dead: his son Ahaziah, after a reign of two years, was dead also; and the crown devolved upon Jehoram, another son of Ahab. This son was not so completely addicted to idols as his parents: he partially suppressed Baal-worship, yet continued the worship of the two calves of Jeroboam, which had indeed become an essential characteristic of the State policy of the kingdom of the ten tribes. Jehoram found it necessary to begin a war against Moab, which had rebelled against the Israelitish dominion. Every reader of the Old Testament history must be somewhat familiar with the Moabitish character. These people were the descendants of Lot. They were therefore the kindred of the children of Abraham; the country on the other side of Jordan and of the

Dead Sea belonged to them; and Moses was forbidden to molest them when he attacked the Canaanitish tribes. But the Moabites, not content with the inhumanity of refusing Israel a peaceable and even gainful passage through their territories (Deut. xxiii. 3, *seq.*) first hired Balaam to curse the people, and then, by the advice of that bad man, led Israel into evil, and brought upon both nations the wrath of Jehovah. The Moabites from this time forward are numbered among the most hostile of the nations around Israel, and frequent wars were the result of their mutual antipathies. In the weak period of the Judges, Israel was subject to Moab (Judg. iii. 14), but in the stronger days of David, Moab was subdued and rendered tributary. When the kingdom was divided the Moabites were made subject to the kingdom of the ten tribes. Perhaps the weakness of the throne in the days of Ahab first emboldened them to throw off the yoke and refuse the customary tribute. Ahab was a warlike prince, but his power was crippled, partly by the religious persecutions which he madly waged against his own subjects, partly by the divine judgments upon the land for idolatry, and partly by the fierce wars he was obliged to carry on with Syria. The tribute imposed upon Moab was large: some judge it was not annual, but paid upon the accession of a new king in Israel. The twenty-two years of Ahab's reign had so weakened his kingdom that Moab correctly judged that his son

Ahaziah would be unable to enforce this claim. So they refused to pay. Two years afterward that weak prince left the throne to his brother, and Moab still proving rebellious, Jehoram made preparations to compel their submission.

At this time Jehoshaphat was the king of Judah. He was one of the best of their kings, but is censured in the Scriptures because he entered into close alliances with the idolatrous family of Ahab. First we find him joining cordially with Ahab in his war against the Syrians; then marrying his son to a daughter of Ahab; now becoming an ally with Jehoram, and perhaps uniting at this same period in a naval expedition, which, however, resulted in a disaster, their vessels being all shipwrecked on the Red Sea, 2 Chron. xx. 37. It is likely that this new alliance took place the next year after Jehoshaphat had himself obtained a signal triumph over the Moabites and the Ammonites, as recorded in 2 Chron. xx. That victory had weakened the Moabites, at the same time that it made Jehoshaphat more ready to join the king of Israel in this new expedition. He brought with him the auxiliary forces of the king of Edom, which was at that time subject to Judah.

There seems to have been another reason of some interest leading to the closer intercourse of the two nations at this time and their alliance in this war against Moab. In 2 Kings ii. 17, Jehoram, the king of Israel, is said to have come to the throne "in the second year of Jehoram the son of Jehoshaphat, because he (*i. e.*, his predecessor and brother, Ahaziah) had no son." But in 2 Kings iii. 1, this same Jehoram is declared to have begun his reign in the eighteenth year of Jehoshaphat. It would appear from comparing various passages that because of his father's sore infirmities (2 Chron. xvi. 12), Jehoshaphat was for a time associated with his father on the throne, and that he associated with himself his son Jehoram in the rule of Judah. So then there were two kings named Jehoram—one the son and successor of Ahab in Israel; the other the son and associate of Jehoshaphat in Judah. Jehoram, king of Israel, came to the throne in the second year of the associated reign of the kings of Judah, but in the eighteenth year of Jehoshaphat's reign. Now as Jehoshaphat's son had married the daughter of Ahab (2 Chron. xxi. 6), it follows that the two Jehorams were brothers-in-law. Such relationship would naturally bind the two kingdoms together more closely. But indeed all this was to the great injury of Judah. More harm than good came of intimacy with Ahab's house. Jehoshaphat had already suffered defeat at Ramoth-Gilead for his alliance with the king of Israel; here he puts his entire army in great peril in their march against Moab; and his son Jehoram after his father's death turned from his father's good ways to do after the manner of his wife's family. We may well wonder at Jehoshaphat, that he was willing to bring such danger to the throne of Judah as to marry his son into such a family, and thus place a daughter of Jezebel in the palaces of Jerusalem.

Various conjectures are made as to the route taken by the allied armies in advancing against Moab. It may have been adopted because the nearest advance would lead them past the strong fortifications of Ramoth-Gilead, where the combined forces of Jehoshaphat and Ahab had been defeated a few years before, and which were still held by the Syrians. Or it may have been for the purpose of securing more completely the doubtful fidelity of the Edomites, who did throw off the yoke of Judah under Jehoshaphat's successor (2 Chron. xxi. 8), or to prevent these doubtful allies from passing through the territories of Judah.* But, whatever may have been the reason for their movement, the three kings, instead of immediately crossing the Jordan and advancing against Moab, passed into a wilderness region south of Judah, and went a seven days' march, where the entire army was in danger of perishing with thirst. In this extremity the king of Israel knew not which way to turn. He speaks of the calamity as a judgment from the Lord, but is not used to asking relief at his hands. But Jehoshaphat was a pious prince, and accustomed to ask counsel from the prophets of the Lord. Indeed the victory he had gained but the year before over the Moabites and their allies had been

* Smith's Dict., art. Moab.

given him in the hour of his weakness by the great mercy of God; and this experience teaches him how to seek succour from him who gave it before.

Knowing well the characteristics of the house of Ahab, he asked not simply for a prophet, but for a prophet of the Lord. He was told that Elisha the son of Shaphat, "who poured water upon the hands of Elijah, was there." Perhaps Jehoshaphat had not heard of Elisha, but Elijah was well known to him, and he had doubtless heard of his translation. Yet it is quite likely that he had heard of Elisha, and was ready to recognize at once his prophetic character. The Orientals are greatly averse to using water that has already been used. Hence they rarely dip their hands into any but running water, and they usually wash by having the water poured upon the hands; this is therefore the duty of an attendant, and the phrase here signifies this. Elisha had been the servant, but is now the successor of Elijah. Before honour is humility. It is related of one of the most excellent modern missionaries to China that when he appeared before the committee of the London Missionary Society, some of the ministers, in their great anxiety to send out only worthy men, did not think him prepared to be a missionary, but offered to send him out if he would go as an assistant to the missionaries. The noble and devoted man replied that he was ready to go in any capacity if he could only be engaged in the work. Upon missionary ground he was willing to be a hewer of wood or a drawer of water to build up the temple of God. With such a spirit we need not wonder to know that he became a most efficient labourer, one of the most valuable of their missionaries in that country.

We do not know how Elisha came to be within reach of the kings, that they might consult with him in this emergency. We do not know whether or not we are to understand that he had accompanied the armies and was then actually in its camp. It is *possible* he was not there; but the armies had some supplies, and by rapid journeys, such as an army could not take, the kings might reach him. But it is *more likely* that in the good providence of God he was then in the camp, and it is not much to the credit of the king of Israel that he did not even know of his presence. It would have been better if these kings had consulted the Lord's will before they began this enterprise, rather than now in their time of extremity. Yet, alas! thus it is too often with our poor human nature. Pious men like Jehoshaphat, and wicked men like Jehoram, are prone to forget God in prosperity and to seek after him when they are full of troubles. So men learn to associate God with sorrows, bereavements and calamities, and separate their joys, successes and pleasures from all thoughts of religion and his service. But the fault of this belongs to themselves. From many a sorrow would men be saved if they set the Lord always before them; in many a joy would men find larger and better pleasure if they recognized God as the Giver of it. Our sorrows often come in the divine faithfulness, and to keep us from an utter forgetfulness of God. If we remembered God and our duty in the day of prosperity, we would be spared many a severe stroke now sent to recal our thoughts; if we never wandered from him, we would not feel the chastisements by whose means he brings wanderers back. Human ignorance sometimes, guilty forgetfulness of God sometimes, are the true sources of the deep afflictions which make us desire to seek God, and lead us to ask, with these anxious kings, "Is there not here a prophet of the Lord?"

The king of Israel himself seems to know nothing of Elisha. The information comes from a servant. We know that in the evil court of Ahab and in times of persecution there was a pious Obadiah—faithful to his God while he served a wicked master—saving the lives of the prophets whom the king and Jezebel would destroy. We are not told who this servant was: perhaps he held quite a subordinate place, yet he could say, Here is Elisha. And in their distress the two monarchs respectfully waited upon the prophet. Elisha was a man of mild and quiet demeanour; usually he wears quite a different aspect from the boldness of the elder prophet. Yet there is a dignity in the bearing of Elisha which shows that he well understands the proprieties of his office. Upon this occasion he addresses the king of Israel with a severe faithfulness which at once reminds us of Elijah. He rebukes his idolatrous propensities, and bids him in the time of his distress betake himself to the prophets nourished by Ahab and Jezebel, and still consulted by himself in hours of prosperity. Why should Jehoram honour the prophets of Baal and the golden calves, affect ignorance of Elisha and his services, and then ask Jehovah's aid in a time of real necessity? Yet this was no time for the king of Israel to resent the boldness of the prophet. His conscience told him too plainly that he deserved the reproof; he saw too well that relief could come from no other quarter, and he stood appalled at the fearful calamity that pressed so closely upon them. His answer may be variously understood: "Nay, for the Lord hath called these three kings together." This may mean a renunciation of his idolatrous faith: I will not seek them, for they cannot help. Men often give up their falsehoods in the hour of peril; skeptics are often changed to firm believers when stern death stares them in the face; but such conversions are of doubtful validity, and when the danger passes they laugh at their own fears and relapse to the practice of their former falsehoods. Or he may mean to plead that as there were three kings there, one of whom the prophet regarded, he might, for the sake of all, plead with God for them.

Elisha has at least vindicated the honour of God

by calling especial attention to the helplessness of the prophets whom Jehoram supported. And now he declares solemnly that but for the presence of King Jehoshaphat he would utterly refuse to do anything in the case. It was little to the honour of Jehoshaphat that he was so allied to Ahab's throne. We may wonder that he did not meet with larger evidences of the divine displeasure. And yet we often see as perplexing things in our own time. All around us, in the world, we see persons that profess piety forming alliances, in business or by marriage or in other ways, with those whose religious views are as truly in contrast as in the case of these two monarchs. Sometimes we see the very life of piety eaten out apparently by the influence of these things. Those who once loved the word, the house and the people of God, and were zealous in his service, become gradually estranged from duties and privileges in which they once delighted. It is not marvellous that our associations should lead us astray, but it is wonderful to notice how the long forbearance of God is shown toward his erring people. He deals not with us according to our sin. Had Elisha left Jehoshaphat to reap the fruit of his own folly, we might esteem this the evidence of Jehovah's displeasure upon his defection. But how much may God's *faithful* servants hope for his protection when he interposes to save even an *inconsistent* one!

Elisha called for a minstrel, that by the tones of

the sacred harp he may be prepared for his duties. We do not understand the ordinary—much less do we comprehend the extraordinary—influence of music upon the soul. We know that in the mental disorder of King Saul the only relief afforded him was when the young David played for him upon the harp, and the king was refreshed and the evil spirit departed from him, 1 Sam. xvi. 23. So upon another occasion we read of a company of prophets prophesying with a psaltery and other instruments of music before them, 1 Sam. x. 5. That Elisha needed any such preparative shows that the prophetic spirit was not inherent, habitual and continual; he shows himself dependent upon divine influence, and the honour is given to God. And when ministers of the gospel now expect the conversion of souls in dependence upon their own intellectual strength, they find disappointment and go forth like Samson shorn of his great powers. But the faith of the kings must also be put to the test. At the command of the Lord they were to dig ditches in the valley; and the prophet gave promise that though they should see neither clouds nor rain, yet the ditches should be filled with an abundant supply of water. Not only so, but he gave assurance also that they should be victorious over the Moabites. This miracle of Elisha was the reverse of that of Elijah. The former prophet had sent a drought upon the land to destroy; Elisha brings water to save. It was a trial of their faith that they were called upon to use means that seemed inappropriate for the end. Had he bidden them offer sacrifices to propitiate his offended God, had he prayed himself as Elijah had prayed on Carmel, had the rising winds and the gathering clouds betokened the coming storm, they would seem to have some encouragement for their faith. But to bid them dig ditches in a soil where a few deep and scanty wells are scattered at wide distances utterly insufficient for an army, seemed a mockery almost. Yet there was this encouragement to their faith—and we shall meet the same thing again in other miracles of this prophet—that they could do nothing better than obey. They had positively no resources but dependence upon the prophet's word; they ought, then, to try the expedient he suggests. This is not the highest form of faith, but it is infinitely better than despair. And that may have been a long and painful night and an anxious morning to these parching troops as they lay by the arid trenches they had scooped up in the desert, waiting until a new proof was afforded that their deliverance was from Jehovah alone. Just at the hour when in the distant Jerusalem the morning sacrifice was laid upon the altar of the temple, the water filled these trenches and the three armies were saved. To the army of Judah this was proof that their God, by whom they had been delivered a year before at the prayer of Jehoshaphat (2 Chron. xx. 5), was still mighty to save. To the army of Israel it was a reproof, because they had forsaken the Lord God of their fathers and had served gods that could not help.

But that they were all saved from thirst was not the full extent of their deliverance. The water thus provided flowed before the eyes of the Moabites, and in the reflection of the sun seemed to them as red as blood. They took the impression that the allied kings had fallen out and shed each other's blood. This was the more natural, because the victory of Jehoshaphat over Moab, to which we have before referred as happening the previous year, had been gained by just such means. The forces upon the same side, perhaps by some mistake of standards or signals, or some discordance of materials in the vast host, had fallen upon each other. And now the Moabites rapidly hurried forward to take advantage of this. But they met with a fearful defeat. The forces of the united kings pursued them everywhere, destroying the land as the prophet expressly bade them—a command that needs no other vindication than the bare mention of a wicked deed just here recorded.

The king of Moab was finally driven into the strongly fortified city of Kir-hareseth. This is perhaps the same place which Isaiah (xxi.) calls Kir-Moab. "It is a few miles south-east of Ar, on a rocky hill, strongly fortified by nature" (Alexander). It was a place almost impregnable by the ancient modes of siege. In the time of the Crusades it stood four years against the forces of Saladin, and was at last reduced by starvation. Perhaps want of provisions distressed the Moabites, and the king at the head of seven hundred choice men attempted to break through upon that side where the Edomites held guard. Either he feared their valour less than that of the others, or he expected sympathy from Edom, itself a subject and impatient nation. Failing to effect this, the king, grown desperate, publicly offered his own son as a sacrifice upon the wall of the city and in full view of all the armies. Human sacrifices have prevailed, and do still prevail, in different parts of the world. This is man's most fearful testimony of his great guilt and need before his Maker. But this deed excited strong emotions in the witnesses. Horrorstruck at such an act of wickedness, they even took no measures to punish the desperate deed, which seemed itself to betoken the ruin of the Moabitish state, but the entire forces abandoned the siege and returned home.

CHAPTER VII.

THE WIDOW'S OIL MULTIPLIED.

IT seems proper for us to judge that the reputation and influence of the prophet Elisha were increased by the great deliverance wrought for the armies of the three kings. A single expression in the succeeding chapter (2 Kings, iv. 13) implies that a word from him would now be favourably considered by the highest civil and military authorities in the land. This indicates the gradual advance of the work to which Elisha had devoted his life. There is no record of honours bestowed: never man cared less than Elisha for pecuniary rewards; indeed for no personal advantages does this man toil. When he left his father's fields and put his hand to this plough, he may not have anticipated fully a prophet's experience; yet pressed he on in labours whose sole object was to honour God and to bless the souls of men, without a thought of decline or of looking back. Whatever influence or honour he may gain, he uses nothing to advance himself: content with frugal fare, he has no means at his disposal to relieve the wants of even the worthy poor. But happily the sweet charities of life are not dependent upon a man's pecuniary ability. They depend rather upon the spirit he possesses: they who pity the poor are fertile in resources for helping them.

The widow of a certain man—one of the sons of the prophets—had fallen into circumstances of great distress, and applied to Elisha for counsel, if not for relief. The ministers of the Church of God in the time of Zion's greatest zeal and purity have been usually men of lowly circumstances. Let us not think strange of this, especially since we know in the history of piety one illustrious example above all value. The greatest of all preachers was the poorest of men—indeed had not where to lay his head; and *chose* this place in life of all he might assume. Surely this should sanctify an estate of poverty to all his followers for ever after him. There are exceptions honourable, to the poverty of the ministry, where a cheerful and liberal people, grateful for spiritual benefits bestowed, have esteemed the labourer worthy of his hire, and have imparted of their temporal things. And there are exceptions dishonourable, where men have worn the name of Christ's ministers and been greedy of filthy lucre and lording over God's heritage. But let us not think strange of the usual poverty of the ministry, but rather find reason to esteem it better so. There are characteristics eminently fitting for those who are consecrated to spiritual duties that are best secured when the heart is not fastened down to earth by earthly possessions. And in their poverty the ministers of God, like their adorable Master, learn to sympathize with those that are necessitous, and those who need sympathy and aid may make hopeful application at their doors for counsel and relief. Elisha lived upon a prophet's fare, but his heart is awoke by the wants of this distressed family in their hour of trial. Think you that God has deprived his servant of any good thing when he calls forth from him sympathy for the sorrowing and liberality from the depths of poverty—that he exacts brick without straw when he gives so little, yet expects so much? Let us rather judge righteous judgment. They are best prepared for true liberality who are unable to give without thought and self-denial, who must plan judicious kindness for the more effectual relief of the applicants, and who are made to share the joy of the benefaction because they have made the offering at some cost to themselves. We may study Elisha's bounty rather because he himself must depend upon the divine beneficence, and because he thus reminds us that all our efforts to relieve the necessities of our fellow-men are but the rendering back upon our part to God himself of blessings we have received from his hand. For this indeed is the view of our beneficence constantly presented in the sacred Scriptures. "Of thine own do we give thee;" "Freely ye have received, freely give;" "He that oppresseth the poor" or "mocketh the poor reproacheth his Maker" (Prov. xiv. 31; xvii.

51); "He that hath pity upon the poor, lendeth unto the Lord;" and that which he hath given will he pay him again." Prov. xix. 17.

The peculiar distress of his family may lead us to recal some thoughts of the ancient usages respecting debts. According to the common practice of ancient nations, a father had full propriety in his children; he could dispose of them as a part of his property; in many instances he had the power of life and death. As the man could himself be sold to pay his debts, so he could sell himself voluntarily or sell his children, or they could be seized by his creditors and sold. This is still done in some Eastern lands. Under the laws of Greece, until the time of Solon, under the laws of Rome, until gradually milder customs grew up under the emperors, creditors had the right to sell a debtor who was unable to pay. We find similar laws frequently recognized in the Scriptures as existing among the Hebrews. If a man was found stealing, he must make restitution, perhaps to double the the amount stolen, or in default of means to do this he was himself to be sold. Ex. xxii. So in Isa. i. 1, God asks Israel, "To which of your creditors have I sold you?" And he himself replies that by their iniquities they had sold themselves. We find the same law recognized in the parable where our Lord speaks of the unforgiving creditor, Matt. xviii. 25. The early laws of all nations exhibit a greater severity against debtors than can be found in our later forms of civilization. We often hear men complain of the tendency to fraud in business transactions; there is much of forgery, counterfeiting, bankruptcy and overreaching; and we are sometimes tempted to judge harshly of various corruptions in our large cities as the great centres of commerce. And the love of money is the root of all evil; they that have many opportunities of getting rich fall into divers snares and temptations, and corrupt practices will always belong to the dealings of sinful men. As the writer of the book of Ecclesiasticus says, "As a nail sticketh fast between the joinings of the stones, so doth sin stick close between buying and selling," xxvii. 2. Yet though, so long as men are depraved, iniquity may be expected in human dealings, every intelligent man must decide that there is a far higher standard of honest dealing in ordinary business, and a far greater promptness between debtors and creditors among us, than in any previous age of the world. Let any one read the accounts of traffic in pagan lands, civilized or barbarous, and he may see this. For example, in the bazaars of India three merchants may be partners in a single room, but they have not sufficient confidence to trust each other. The door will be fastened with three locks, each man will have his own separate key, and the three partners must be present before either of them can enter. We have cheating in our circles of trade indeed, but there are as honourable and truthful men among our trades of every rank as the earth can afford.

In regard to the Hebrew laws in general, we may say that they are often like the laws of the nations around them, even in cases where we look for quite a difference, but they may have been in every case well adapted to the social standing of the people. The differences between them and those of neighbouring nations are all improvements. The laws regulating debts were milder for their own people in two respects: 1st. A Hebrew could only be sold for seven years, though at the end of that time he could voluntarily become a servant for life, Ex. xxi. 2–6. 2d. Even when sold, no Hebrew could be a slave or a bondman; he must be treated as a hired servant or a sojourner, Lev. xxv. 40. In this regard we may find the laws of God's people more severe than would be approved by the milder spirit of our civilization, but it is remarkable that they were much more humane than similar laws of other ancient nations.

The circumstances of this poor family may enlist our sympathies. Let us understand that this is a case that is no lighter to those who suffer because the custom is familiar in the land. The people around this poor woman may have taken less interest in her lamentable estate because they had often seen families sold for debt, and they may have seen nothing specially cruel in the proceedings of the creditor. Slavery and family separations doubtless seem less flagrant wrongs when they are matters of our familiar observation, yet to the sufferers in every case the evils they must endure are aggravated by this very thing, since sympathy would mitigate the grief it might not be able to relieve. But for familiar evils there is comparatively little sympathy.

The Jews say that this was the widow of Obadiah, who was steward to Ahab, who saved a hundred prophets from Jezebel's persecutions, and who, by reason of this, had become a debtor to the king himself. This is, for several reasons, unlikely. We have no reason to think that Obadiah was a prophet at all; rather we judge that Ahab would not have retained as his steward one who was himself amenable to Jezebel's rage. This is to us an unknown prophet. He was known, however, to Elisha, and doubtless as a man of piety and worth. Perhaps he knew also the circumstances of the family, and how it came to pass that his death left them destitute. It is our duty to relieve suffering, even when folly and guilt have brought men into distress, yet it is no breach of charity to say that we may be far more willing to help the worthy poor. By far the heaviest drafts upon human benevolence are made by the vicious—the danger of wasting our gifts may properly make us careful in bestowing them; but our sympathies should go freely forth when the object of our benefactions is both distressed and deserving. The portion of the prophets in Israel was perhaps very precarious. Theirs was usually a frugal life, and they had seldom much to leave for their children, except that enduring legacy which the wise man praises, Prov. xiii. 22. A good name and the covenant mercy of his God is the inheritance which a good man often leaves to his children's children. And we shall see in this case that God has not forgotten his servant, though his bereaved family are in distress so sore.

We can easily believe that this household has been brought to want neither by imprudence nor prodigality, much less by more discreditable means. This prophet—let his name be what it may—lived in times of severe trial for those who served in the name of Jehovah. The land groaned by reason of its iniquities; the rulers of Israel had cast down the altars, and had exalted Baal, Ashtaroth and the calves of Jeroboam; persecutions had cut off the multitude of true prophets; and famine in the judgments of God had impoverished the people. This prophet may have been too young for a full share in these troubles, running back for a quarter of a century in the history of the land, yet if his two sons were now old enough to aid their mother's faith or to be of much value to their creditor, the father's period of service in the ministry did not fall much behind these troublous times of the State. Considering the circumstances of the family, we must believe that the deceased father entered the ministry in the severe threatenings of the troublous times, undeterred by the frowns of Jezebel, or that he endured the full severity of those terrible days. In either case, all credit to his courage and faith! Lately the times had been more favourable, since the labours of Elijah and Elisha have met with some good success; yet the precarious incomes of the prophets are doubtless much affected by the unsettled condition of affairs, from which recovery was slow. All these things may keep us from judging uncharitably of this family's pecuniary embarrassments. Those who fear God should be careful not to involve themselves in debt; even with prospective ability to pay, great caution should be exercised in this respect; they should do this, not only because honesty demands it, and because their own comfort and well-being are promoted by it, but also because the honour of religion is involved in the reputation of its professors. Yet it is no crime to be poor. Many a worthy man has been involved in such a way as not to implicate his character; and even where we think there has been imprudence, we should be sparing of our censures upon those who may simply be unfortunate.

When God's people are in distress they apply to God's ministers for sympathy and relief. Doubtless this prophet's widow knew that Elisha was too poor to pay her debt, but she wishes his counsel, perhaps also his influence with her creditor. Nor did she apply in vain. Yet we do not suppose that she could anticipate the mode of relief. But we may admire the prophet's method, as teaching us that grand secret of a true benevolence, that it is better for both the giver and the receiver to exercise faith. We must give even when our hands are not full of ready means that can be spared without self-denial; yet we must so give that as much as possible the relief shall call forth the energies of those who receive. By faith, Elisha helps; by faith, the widow is helped; and though we usually overlook the blessing which the prophet received, because our thoughts are chiefly fixed upon the suffering family, it is still true that he who confers a kindness often receives a larger reward than his beneficiary. "Remember the words of the Lord Jesus, how that he said, It is more blessed to give than to receive," Acts xx. 35. Yet see how the prophet wisely calls forth the widow's own resources, efforts and faith. He asks her what she has in the house. In times of destitution we have unthought-of resources; wisdom would draw these out, and they will yield far more than a dejected and stricken heart can think is possible. Grief sometimes unnerves us from planning and doing, though indeed this is neither wise nor right. Many a heart loses its best energies in corroding sorrow, yet never more do we need that they should be well employed in serious, active duties. It is related that the wife of a general wounded in the battle of Pittsburg Landing, hastening to his relief, found him already dead; at first she was overwhelmed with her great grief, but soon, seeing so much distress around her, she began, with all a woman's tenderness, to care for the suffering and dying, and she assuaged her own sorrows while she ministered to theirs. This is our true duty. We may sorrow in our afflictions, but the grief that overlooks pressing and important duties is insubmissive and improper. Changes in our circumstances often develop hidden energies and resources that are greatly profitable. How worthy of our interested study are the orderings of Providence! That is a dark state of affairs indeed upon which Providence can throw no light.

The prophet found that this poor woman had in her house a single vessel of oil. The olives of Palestine are among the most valuable productions of the land. Moses promised the Israelites that they should have "oil out the flinty rock," Deut. xxxii. 13. The olive trees insinuate their roots into the clefts of the hard, rocky soil; they require but little cultivation, and twenty generations of owners may gather the fruits. A single large tree will yield from ten to fifteen gallons of oil in a good season, and an acre will yield a crop worth a hundred dollars.* So important was the gathering of the olives to the interests of the community that it was regulated by law. No man could take the fruit from his own trees until the government issued a proclamation declaring the time of gathering; and then

* The Land and the Book, i. 74.

the entire population turned out to secure the fruit. It is not likely that this poor widow had the right to gather olives as the owner of an acre or even of a tree. But this vessel of oil which she had in her house was perhaps the fruit of her industry; she and her sons may have earned somewhat as labourers in the time of gathering; and it was an express command of Moses that in gathering olives they should not be too careful to collect the berries, but should leave a portion for the stranger, for the fatherless and for the widow, Deut. xxiv. 20. The oil that is to relieve the widow was the product of her own industry. Had she collected it for her own use, either for cooking or for light, she would perhaps have made no mention of it at Elisha's inquiry. The sale of this oil was the meagre provision for the support of her household.

The command of the prophet puts her faith to the test in a double sense. He told her to borrow all the vessels she could of the neighbours, and then to pour out from her vessel of oil into those she had thus borrowed until she had filled them all. Here her faith was tested as to its reality and as to its strength. Unbelief would judge that the prophet did but mock; the oil would empty itself out of her vessel, and then cease to flow. Little faith would say that she need borrow but a few vessels for a purpose like this. We are not led to think that this poor widow consulted any of the friends around her except Elisha, or that she even informed her neighbours of her purpose in borrowing so many vessels. That she kept the entire matter to herself seems rather implied in the direction to shut the door upon herself and her sons while she obeyed the prophet's command. We have here a very important suggestion respecting our plain duties. Let us not seek for counsellors when we are in no perplexity; let us do, not consult, when our duty is plain. Paul tells us that when he received the command of God immediately he "conferred not with flesh and blood." When Abraham received the command of God, he rose early in the morning to do the painful bidding. "Conferring with flesh and blood"—*i. e.*, taking counsel with man, may be proper and valuable in cases where we are to ascertain what our duty is, but when our duty is known, it is wisdom to go promptly forward; we lose far more than we gain by our consulting with others. The matter is not one for advice, but for ready faith and prompt obedience. Had this woman asked the advice of others after the counsel she had received from Elisha, she would doubtless have found many timid to credit his words, many utterly incredulous, and but a few to encourage her faith. The world of men are averse from God. If we follow either the opinions or the practice of the mass of the people around us, we will surely never secure the divine approbation. Most men are careless of religion, unbelieving toward God, indifferent toward their own souls. Even serious minds often falter in their faith.

In the plain pathway of duty men should depend less upon others. We truly meet our responsibilities when we remember our personal accountability to God. Taking everything into the account, every man who seriously studies his responsibilities will feel their force and know their obligations upon him as no other person can for him. We easily see how this is when we think of anything else than our religious duties. What kind of management would any man make of his private business as a merchant, a mechanic or a farmer if he depended rather upon the judgment of other people than upon his own? Do they know his affairs as he knows them? Do they take as deep an interest in them? In case of any failure, do they feel the loss as he would feel it, or are they as careful in advising his important actions as they would be if the case was their own? Certainly these inquiries answer themselves. We have a prosperous community in proportion as every man sees to his own affairs; let every man learn of others, but let no man lay aside his own responsibility. Ask advice in the hour of perplexity, but in cases where you know well enough the path of right go forward directly in it.

The prophet's words were plain, and this poor woman believed and obeyed. She sent her sons to borrow vessels of their acquaintances and neighbours.

We hope the children of the prophet's household were like-minded with their believing mother, and entered heartily into the work. And when they had gathered either all they could procure or all their faith thought would be needful, she shut the door of her house and the wonder of deliverance began. One son gave her the empty vessels; from her full pot she poured the golden stream until they were full of oil; and the other son set the full vessels aside. All the vessels in the house were filled, and then the oil stayed. The narrative is so brief, and there is so little declaration of the result, that we do not know what judgment to form of the strength of her faith. Whether her sons stopped borrowing because they thought they had enough, or because their faith feared that even all they had might not be filled, or because they really could borrow no more, we are not told; but of this much we are informed—and it seems to intimate that her faith was strong indeed—that the supply was not only enough to pay the indebtedness, but also to provide something for the support of the family afterward. The prophet directed her to pay the debt and live upon the balance. Yet is it not significant that the oil stayed only because there were no more vessels to fill?

Are there not here lessons of the divine Hand, as the same may be traced in grace within us and in providence all around us? Wonderful it seems to be, that vessel of ever-flowing oil! Yet do we disbelieve the greater wonders all about us whose mysteries we cannot explain? We are familiar with other and greater wonders; we never think of questioning them: do we really understand them any better? It is quite appropriate for us to liken the oil of the widow to the grace of God as given to believers—at once their release from a more fearful indebtedness, and their livelihood for a spiritual, even an unending, existence. We may make this comparison the rather because in the instructive vision of one of the prophets the oil giving light upon the golden candlestick is typical of the Spirit's influence to promote the piety of the Church of God, Zech. iv. The golden-coloured oil empties into the lamp that its light may burn brightly, for piety in the Church and in the believer's heart is not by might nor by power, but by the Spirit of the Lord. And let our faith but find room for the continual outpouring of this holy oil, and the supply will never cease. We are not straitened in God, but in ourselves.

And this miracle is designed to remind us of the inexhaustible resources of divine providence for the relief of the suffering poor. Yet why indeed should we speak of the poor, since in his sight "the rich and the poor meet together," and every man living is at all times dependent? But it impresses us more when we see the circumstances of distress in which many are involved. We are often led to wonder that God allows his people to fall into such difficulties, that their troubles often arise out of their very efforts to do right, and that they are long in trouble and are reduced to deep extremities. It almost seems to us either inconsistent with the divine faithfulness, on the one hand, or, upon the other, an evidence of some secret iniquity in the afflicted persons which we had not suspected. But divine wisdom judges otherwise. Even if the Jewish story told by Josephus concerning this prophet's widow was correct, we are but reading a narrative that may find a thousand like it in the history of God's suffering people: nor may we even truly say that God has forgotten if no prophet comes to grant a wonderful release. The principles of the divine administration remain the same: there never exists a case of grief among his people that God does not pity, though the methods he devises for relief are infinitely various. Josephus says not only that this was the widow of Obadiah, but that the debt had been contracted in his efforts to feed the persecuted prophets. For reasons of infinite wisdom, God may allow his people to fall into deep straits when they are innocent—when their zeal for him is the occasion of their trouble. He here shows himself a helper of the poor and dependent, that we may learn to trust him in every extremity.

Two things seem chiefly aimed at in the plans of divine providence when we are reduced to dependence and helplessness. The first is the trial of our faith; the second is the showing forth of the divine glory. Unquestionably, this trial of faith is far more severe in some cases than in others, but we are assured that all our temptations and trials are adapted to us; they are such as we are able to bear; and with them there is afforded also a way of escape, 1 Cor. x. 13. This is in the divine faithfulness. It is implied in our times of trial that as a matter of fact we do not know what is before us, but all the while the path of our duty may be very plain, and we may very well know the principles by which we should be governed. *Negatively* we know that our severest straits do not justify our transgressing the divine law. When this poor widow was so deeply indebted that her family was about to be dissolved, this afforded no reason for resorting to fraud or falsehood, or any breach of the divine law, for their relief. Many persons—some without any necessity, and some by an apparent necessity—live by the earnings of unlawful industry. They engage in an injurious business; they labour on the Sabbath in express violation of the divine law; they misrepresent the goods they sell to increase their profits; they are unfaithful to their employers through their own ease or indolence. These things are as really, if not as grossly, distrusting Providence as if a man should support his family by robbery, and should excuse his wrong by declaring, "We must live." Faith in the providence of God forbids the wilful pursuit of wrong. Presumption, not faith, is idle or wicked. There is a nobler life than that of the body, and our highest aim should be to promote it. This is the very point of our Lord's reply to the tempter, when he would have him distrust the dealings of Providence: "Man shall not live by bread alone, but by every word that proceedeth out of the mouth of God." No principle is plainer for man's guidance while he depends upon his God than that stooping to evil is distrust of Providence, and that to know anything as evil is a sufficient proof that we are to avoid it.

But a true dependence on Providence is *positive*, and it uses all due means to reach a lawful end. Trust in God is sometimes a patient waiting on his will when the believing soul does nothing but wait; yet to justify such a position we must be unable to do anything. Prayer itself must never stand alone save where we can do nothing but pray. Any indisposition to do the plain orderings of duty is so far a disqualification for acceptable prayer. This poor widow cried to God's servant for relief, yet not because she is indisposed for exertion. She had gathered what oil she could before she applied for help. She is ready to do his bidding, even though a new and strange faith is involved in the command. Usually the path of duty is quite as plain as our readiness to go forward. We are perplexed, not because we know not what to do, but we fear we should not gain the end we desire even by doing our duty. Just here let us have faith in God. Should his will call us to patience and suffering, let us in well-doing commit our souls to him as to a faithful Creator. We need not fear, in even a painful path, where duty leads. God knows how to deliver. He who miraculously helped the prophet's widow can still help those who put their trust in him, by means as honouring to himself as any miracle. Many who never saw such a wonder have yet an experience as truly honouring to the divine Hand.

Happy for ourselves and honouring to God is our calm and constant trust in his care. Why should we take anxious thought for to-morrow? We cannot hasten or delay to-morrow's coming; we cannot help or hinder the responsibilities that to-morrow must bring: we are all dependence in our most zealous and active engagements. Let us trust God, and prove our trust by keeping back our hearts and hands from things evil and presumptuous —by asking divine counsel in every perplexity; and, while we ask strength for every duty, by humbly and earnestly doing his holy will. But remember, it is not *trusting* God—it is *distrusting* him—when we neglect our plain duties, and any apparent dependence while we are needlessly idle is not true faith. This widow could do little to save her household from bondage, but the little she could she did. The pouring forth of that oil was nothing effective, yet as the appointed means of deliverance it was indispensable. How feeble are a sinner's prayers! Yet he who will not pray must perish.

CHAPTER VIII.

THE SHUNAMITE.

IT is enough to commend the duty of hospitality to every Christian household to read the apostolic injunction, "Be not forgetful to entertain strangers, for thereby some have entertained angels unawares," Heb. xiii. 2. Doubtless he refers especially to Abraham and Lot—perhaps also to Manoah, who received kindly those who afterward proved indeed to be angels. See Gen. xviii. 2; xix. 1; Judges xiii. 19. But when the woman of Shunem treated courteously the prophet Elisha, she prepared the way for a blessing upon her household, and many a humble family in the Church has been largely blessed in imitating the hospitality of other times. A wise and godly guest more than compensates his entertainers for the cost and inconvenience of his sojourn with them; and the sweet savour of his memory may abide in the house long after he has taken his departure.

Eastern lands are famed for the attention paid to the wants of strangers. No obligations are regarded as more sacred or are more carefully observed than those of hospitality. Plato, in his

Dialogues upon the Laws, declares that the avenging deities are specially severe against inhospitality, because a stranger, being destitute of friends, is an object of greater pity to men and to the gods. Plato, Op. vi. 144, 145, (Bk. v., De Legibus). The Arabs of the present day are profuse in their kindness to strangers; even the Hindús extend the duty of hospitality to enemies by their proverb, that "a tree does not withdraw its shade even from the wood-cutter;" and we are sufficiently familiar with the African women, whose song for the poor white man is so touchingly given by Mungo Park. Doubtless these habits of hospitality were more needful in Eastern lands, where hotels in our sense of the word were wholly unknown; but the Scriptures recognize the duty as one that should not be laid aside by Christians, though its extent and necessity is in a great degree changed by a different aspect of society. If Job, vindicating his uprightness, numbered this among his virtues, "The stranger did not lodge in the street, but I opened my doors to the traveller" (xxxi. 32), we also, for its own sake and in obedience to inspired directions, should cultivate this virtue. But the Apostle's words direct us to maintain the proper spirit of entertainers while we do the external duty: "Use hospitality one to another without grudging," 1 Pet. iv. 9.

We have suggested that several schools of the prophets seem to have been established by Elijah and Elisha in different parts of the land. We can hardly decide that Elisha at this period of his ministry had any one place of residence, but he visited these schools in succession, perhaps with some degree of regularity. In journeying from Samaria* to Mount Carmel he had occasion to pass through the village of Shunem. Here dwelt an aged man, possessed of considerable property, in whose house the prophet was kindly received. And here is the test of the true spirit of hospitality, that as his journeys that way were frequent, his entertainers, instead of becoming weary of their guest, made preparations to put him more at his ease, to show him that he was ever welcome, and to afford him a quiet retreat suited to his own tastes, where he could come and go at his own pleasure. The suggestion came from the woman of the house, who, it seems, was much younger than her husband; but doubtless all was with his cordial approbation. A room was built expressly for Elisha; it was comfortably furnished according to the simple habits of the times; and the prophet was given to understand that it was entirely at his disposal as often as he might see fit to tarry with the family as their honoured guest. This indeed was using "hospitality without grudging."

If this household in Shunem teaches us the duties of a host and the virtue of hospitality, let the prophet also teach us the answering duties of a

* Here seems to have been his residence at a later date, 2 Kings v. 3.

guest and the virtue of gratitude. This is the excellent arrangement of our social life, that there is action and reaction in all we are and in all we do. Unhappily, sin often begets sin—"grievous words stir up anger." Happily, every kindness reflects back its own image; "Give and it shall be given to you." Indeed it is in our power to do much to check evil by returning good for it; "a soft answer turneth away wrath." But we are quite inexcusable when kindness awakens no answering feeling. In a right-minded man gratitude is easily called forth. The prophet is grateful for the kindness of this woman, and is desirous of making her some suitable return. He therefore consulted with his servant Gehazi, whose name now first appears in the narrative, and of whom we will have some further things to say. He first offered her that he would make any request she might desire of the civil or military authorities. This incidentally proves that Elisha's services find some appreciation in Israel, though he is ever indisposed to use his influence for any personal advantage. When this proposal seemed not to suit the case, the gratitude of the prophet still pursues his object to give some return for the Shunamite's kindness. A truly grateful spirit is not satisfied with the mere offer of thanks, but is really desirous of bestowing benefit.

Still another lesson—as hard to learn as any that belongs to our earthly life—is found in the Shunamite's reply—a lesson of contentment. For various reasons, few persons are entirely contented with their lot in life. Though it is not hard to find many all around us who have a harder lot than our own—though we know that all our way in life is ordered in the infinite wisdom of God's holy providence—though experience teaches us that nothing is to be gained by fretfulness and repining—few men are really contented.

Possibly, this Shunamite expresses a delicate sensibility because the prophet thinks of making any return for her kindness, as though her hospitality was not wholly disinterested, and needed some expression from him as its reward. But when she says, "I dwell among my own people," we rather understand her to declare that she desired no preferment, no change, no reputation beyond wnat she already had; around her already were all the enjoyments, all the friends, all the substance she wished for upon earth; and that she did not send out her thoughts in longings for things not given her in the divine allotments. Happy woman! who has learned the lesson of true happiness, and who knows when she is well off! Happy they who learn from her or with her that true happiness is not to be found by departing from our sphere of life, by desiring new circles of friends or by longing for new engagements, but by the curbing of undue desires and by contentment with such things as we have!

Contentment with our lot in life is a duty, both

as we look at the providence of God, which orders all our affairs, and as we regard our happiness, which depends less upon our circumstances than upon the disposition we ourselves maintain. Two things doubtless make the exercise of a proper spirit more difficult on the part of man: The *first* is that we are sinners, and therefore naturally disposed to find pleasure in earthly things; we must therefore be disappointed and restless. The *next* is that our powers are in constant development; it is therefore natural and lawful for us to desire to advance in our acquirements. The enjoyments of life, the possessions of life, we may lawfully desire; and if we overstep not the bounds assigned by Providence, we may desire advancement, yet not be discontented. To possess desires and yet to restrain our desires* within due bounds seems to be the very thing meant by a pious content. When troubles befal, let us not murmur; when burdens oppress, let us serenely sustain them; when comforts fail, let us meekly resign them; let us not be vexed and impatient, even if our situation is not in every respect agreeable; let us make the best of those things we have, and keep back our imaginations from the possible changes which, in the distance, may seem so desirable.

A light and cheerful disposition, disposed to look upon the bright side of things, is not contentment; nor is that uniform indifference which seems to care

* Dwight's Theol., iii. 528.

little for either the sorrows or the joys of life. Two virtues must abide together to secure the full exercise of either in the sight of God. So writes the Apostle: "Godliness with contentment is great gain." Many reasons, indeed, and such as the Apostle himself urges, may induce even those who are not godly to be still content with such things as they have. For why should we catch after the things we can hold with so feeble a grasp? "For we brought nothing into this world, and it is certain we can carry nothing out; and having food and raiment, we should be therewith content." But reasons drawn from the government of God should be more prevailing. On the one hand, we should be kept from envious or covetous thoughts because others are more prosperous than ourselves; we should notice that true happiness depends but little upon external circumstances; and we should recognize that any possible changes will fail to bring contentment to those who are disposed to be murmuring. On the other hand, we should acknowledge that in the wise and supreme government of God nothing comes to pass but for good reasons; we should find it our interest and happiness, while we press earnestly on in the pathway of duty, to acquiesce in all the orderings of Providence; a just conviction of our unworthiness to receive the mercies already bestowed, and the disposition to mark how numerous are the bounties of the divine Hand, should be added to the moderation of our desires;

while a wise observation of men and things all around us should teach us that "a man's life consisteth not in the abundance of the things which he possesseth," and that indeed some of the happiest of our race are those who have learned the lessons of sorrow and disappointment.

If we may often say that virtue is its own reward, we may so speak especially of this grace. A happy disposition is a great possession; but Christian contentment, that bids us enjoy with peaceful acquiescence the orderings of Providence, is better far. It preserves us from temptations that are inseparable from the inordinate longings of pride, ambition and covetousness; it bids us enjoy what we have, and forbids restless envy and graspings after things we may not have; it enables us better to discharge the various duties we owe to society; and it is itself acceptable to God. We do not know in what school the Shunamite learned her lesson of contentment. We shall see her in changed circumstances, in both bereavement and exile, and she may teach us then to conform to our changing times, but she does not exhibit any inconsistency from her present mind. If the regular, lawful prosecution of our duties in life, or the unsought orderings of divine providence, bring any changes, if we should change our home or our engagements, or our sphere of service, we should be conformed, as far as possible, to our new condition. But true contentment checks our restless longings for change; forbids us to indulge in fretful repinings, which irritate our own hearts while they are rebellious against Providence; enables us cheerfully to support the trials which usually attend every change in life; finds reasons for gratitude in the most unexpected events; and even when things are undesirable, points us forward, both to earthly reverses which could easily make things worse than they now are, and to future prospects when God's people shall be fully satisfied for ever.

Godliness with contentment is great gain, for they who have a God on whom they may rely cannot really want any good thing.

Yet though the Shunamite has no wants to express to her illustrious guest and desires no such changes as man could give, it does not follow that her happiness could not be improved by the gifts which a greater than man can bestow. The prophet's servant has noticed not only the absence of children in the household, but that the blessing of a child would be highly valued by the family. We need not remark upon the peculiar anxiety manifested among the Hebrew people for offspring, or trace this simply to the national expectation of the coming Christ, since indeed in all ages and all lands "a babe in a house is a well-spring of pleasure." It is in the orderings of a kind Providence that a child born in a family is a bond of new affection for the parents, calling out new elements of character not only toward the child, but also toward each other and all that are about them. It was not inconsistent with a contented mind that this woman was grateful for the prophet's assurance. We have already said that there are lawful longings for our comfort and welfare which are within the proper definition of a contented disposition.

But how true it is that our heaviest trials in life often spring from our dearest comforts! Indeed lessons of submission are only possible when our hearts are deeply interested in the object of our bereavement. A few years afterward, when the child had grown large enough to go forth with his father to the field, he had perhaps a new stroke. "I know by experience," says a missionary writing from the same section of the country, "that this valley glows like a furnace in harvest-time."* They carried him to his mother. But here we have the sad scene that has darkened the doors of so many households—well in the morning, dead in his mother's arms by noon! How little can the best things of earth stay or alleviate the advances of sorrow! It is no help now that she was a great woman and that she dwelt among her own people. And it is no hindrance to the lessons she would now teach all Bible-readers; for we do not look now upon her as the rich lady of Shunem, but as the mother bereaved of her only child.

And now her thoughts turn toward the prophet who had promised her this son. Doubtless, she had

* The Land and Book, ii. 177.

heard that Elijah had restored to life the son of the widow of Zarephath, and Elisha possesses the same double-portioned spirit. Whether her faith at once grasped the possibility that thus he would do for her, or whether she turned to him for relief without anticipating what the man of God would do, we cannot tell. But no sooner had the great grief fallen upon her than she is desirous of laying it before Elisha. With her husband's consent—not at once granted, because he knew no reason why she should go—she rode to Mount Carmel, where she knew the prophet was. The distance was ten or twelve miles, and lest the servant, fearing she might be over-fatigued, might not drive fast enough, she bid him not spare the beast through any consideration for her. Elisha saw her coming in haste, recognized her, and instantly feared some calamity. He sent Gehazi to meet her. But she gave a brief answer to the servant, and in her great grief pressed on to the feet of the prophet.

Dr. Thomson says that the whole scene is natural —not only the embrace of the prophet's feet, but the answer she gives—and that similar scenes and replies may often be observed among the people still residing there. While indeed habit may use gestures and language which mean very little, yet the language she uses is so appropriate and pious that we are unwilling to believe that the Shunamite did not feel just as she speaks, and so we enter truly into the spirit of her own words. She cannot repress the anguish of her soul that she has so suddenly lost her only child, yet she recognizes a higher Hand than that of man, and submissively declares, "It is well." The very fact that she came to see the prophet shows that this is so. This is the very spirit of Job—Just because affliction springs not from the dust, just because troubles arise not by chance, I will seek unto God. There would be no propriety in seeking consolation or considering the nature and design of our sorrows if in fact they had no design. Our afflictions are not calamities or casualties—they are chastenings and providences. It is well; they have come forth from the divine hand. She comes to the servant of the Lord, because, while she recognizes the divine sovereignty in the sudden stroke that has befallen her, she hopes also for some relief from Him who sent the stroke.

The prophet deeply sympathized with his afflicted friend. He saw that she acted under some heavy sorrow, but the Lord had not revealed to him its cause. He soon learned that her son was the source of her grief. He immediately sent Gehazi forward to lay his staff upon the face of the child. Doubtless this staff was a mark of his prophetic office. So Moses had a staff which he bore from the deserts of Sinai, and which he often used in working wonders. Why the staff did not secure the end we can but guess. Perhaps it would have sufficed to raise the child, and to send it forward shows the strong faith of the prophet. But before Gehazi had reached the house and laid the staff upon the child's face, Elisha had already changed his purpose and was himself coming in person. The faith of the prophet was strong enough to work this miracle without his own presence, but the poor mother wishes now that he should accompany her; she will not leave him, and in sympathy with her, and in condescension to the weakness of her faith, he does otherwise than his first intention. It may have been some trial for her faith, scarcely for his, that Gehazi, having laid the staff upon the child's face, met them to say that there was neither voice nor hearing, and that he was not awaked.

The prophet raised the child to life again and delivered him to his mother. But great a thing as this was, we cannot read the narrative without recalling that a greater than Elisha in later days wrought still more wondrously. It was fitting that the Lord of all the prophets should have the pre-eminence over all his servants. In all these resurrections there was doubtless an instructive intimation that the faith which Elisha preached had the power of raising the dead soul to spiritual life. And in view of the fact that the wonders of grace are still wrought where the same blessed gospel is proclaimed, that believing parents may still come to the God of Israel and ask for the life of their children, and that this is a greater and more permanent work than that wrought by Elisha, why should we not exercise a like faith for these better things? We may rank this Shunamite with those believers whose triumphs of faith the Apostle names. "Women received their dead raised to life again." And if the question be asked, "Why does not God now hear the prayer of bereaved parents, and warrant the exercise of our faith for a restoration to life? the answer would not be proper which did not remind us that God may change his dealings with his people, but he never changes the principles upon which his dealings have ever been founded. The God that ever pitied, always pities: "like as a father pitieth his children, so the Lord pitieth them that fear him." Not because he does not pity does he no longer send relief in this form. We may trust him that the change is wisely made; we may believe that relief will come in every time of trouble; we should bring the spiritual wants of our families before him and plead for their relief. Perhaps in after years this son of the Shunamite heard this story of his mother's faith, learned that through her he had been restored to life, and loved her memory the more because he was thus indebted to her. How many children live now upon the earth, how many have passed to heaven, who owe to a mother's faith and a mother's prayers a blessing far greater than a child's restoration to the cares and duties of this earthly life!—even a preparation for the service of God and an everlasting life.

At a later time in the history (2 Kings viii. 1–6) we read that this woman again experienced the gratitude of Elisha. Knowing by inspiration that the land was about to be visited by a famine, he forewarned her to seek refuge abroad. Perhaps by this time her husband was dead, as no mention is made of him. We know not why the prophet bade her go to the land of the Philistines, but she was there seven years. Just before her return, Elisha had conferred new benefits upon Israel, and stood in high favour with the king of the land. The Shunamite could no longer say, "I dwell among my own people;" and now she might have been quite willing to be spoken for to the chief captain or the king. Yet we may judge from her previous character that she was ready to commit her way to the Lord. She is now under the necessity of appealing to the king for the restoration of her property, which under the common law of that land was confiscated upon her removal. But little likelihood generally exists of having such property restored, unless upon the mediation of some influential person.* She makes no application to the prophet, who, it may be, was not within her reach. But providentially she applied at a very favourable moment. Just then the king had been inquiring of Gehazi, the prophet's servant, what miracles his master had wrought. Gehazi was then suffering under the heavy punishment of his sin. Perhaps

* The Land and the Book, ii. 178.

it had wrought in him a salutary change; and he is more disposed than ever to work a good work. At the very moment when he told the king that Elisha had restored the Shunamite's son to life, she made her appearance to ask the restoration of her lands. Gehazi recognized her at once, and added greatly to the interest of his narrative before the king by declaring that this was the woman and her son of whom he had just been speaking. Thus the king had the opportunity of hearing the full account from her own lips; and so much was he interested in the whole matter that he readily gave the order for the restitution of her lands and all the fruits from the time she had left. Doubtless she thought that this again was no chance matter, but said with Solomon, "The king's heart is in the hand of the Lord as the rivers of water; he turneth it whithersoever he will," Prov. xxi. 1. The providence of God is to be recognized in our mercies, not only when we cannot, but also when we think we can, see the steps by which our deliverances are wrought. The Shunamite would look upon the prophet Elisha and upon the leper Gehazi and upon the wicked king of Israel as but instruments in the hand of God to do his holy purposes.

And still he doeth all things well. The course of life may not always run smoothly: joy and sorrow, plenty and famine may alternate with each other in our experience; but no man commits his way truly to God, submits meekly to his orderings, obeys his injunctions and trusts his care, who shall be disappointed. How can things be otherwise than well, how can we indulge our griefs insubmissively, how can we doubt that even unexpected and heavy afflictions shall work eventually for our good, when we consider the government of God, when we rely upon his promises, and when we so submit ourselves to him as to make him our Guide, our Hope, our Trust?

Let the Shunamite teach us that bread cast upon the waters may be found after many days. Truly she may be reckoned among those who have exercised hospitality and entertained an angel unawares. She had no thought that the kindness she so cheerfully showed to Elisha would bring in so large returns. And indeed is it not often so with us? Our actions are seeds, and we know not whether shall prosper either this or that. Some evil thing done, some evil word spoken, may start into fearful prominence to disturb our happiness for many days, or some trifling good may be the beginning of many comforts through more than earthly life.

CHAPTER IX.

THE SYRIAN LEPER.

WE should never allow ourselves to lose sight of the significancy of the scriptural miracles. This truly is an important and permanent value belonging to them—that they remain as instructive in the record of them now as they were advantageous in the day they were wrought. Indeed there is a sense in which we may claim that we get larger profit from the wonders of ancient times than did the men who witnessed them. They were doubtless more impressed with marvels that were wrought before their eyes than we are with the familiar record; yet there is proof of divine power here to us as well as to them; and because we may see the entire train of scriptural miracles as they are connected with one great system, the principles that pervade the whole, the ends aimed at in the divine orderings, and the lessons taught us by their especial significance, it seems proper to class these great things of the Scripture among the instructions which later ages can better understand than the earlier.

We may sometimes be at a loss to see the exact

purpose of every wonder here recorded. This should not be thought strange. Doubtless everything that God has made in the world around us has its purpose, its wise and beneficent purpose. But is the most intelligent man prepared to say what is the divine design in so many various forms of living and inanimate things, in so many varied dealings of the providence of God? Thousands of things help make up this world; thousands of events are connected with the onward progress of the world's history; we cannot decide what would be the loss if this or that had no existence, yet we may believe that all things have their wise purpose. And, whatever perplexity may attend the effort to understand everything, the general beneficence of the divine dealings is manifest. And so judge we of these miraculous records. In the time of a famine, Elisha, upon two occasions, relieved the necessities of the sons of the prophets. The fare of his disciples, always frugal, was especially scanty at such a time as this. They gathered for themselves from the fields what they could for their humble meals; and, "better skilled in divinity than in natural philosophy," as Matthew Henry quaintly remarks, they gathered an apparently edible gourd that proved bitter and poisonous.* The prophet healed the dangerous food. So he multiplied miraculously a few loaves of bread to supply the entire company of scholars at one of these

* The Land and the Book, ii. 179.

seminaries, where, we are incidentally told, were a hundred men. We are at no loss to see the significance of these miracles. God cares not only for his prophets, but for his poor, in times of deep necessity; he delivers them from dangers into which they have ignorantly gone; and when scanty gifts are offered in a time of distress, he multiplies the things that are freely bestowed from the poverty of their brethren, so that a small gift may accomplish far more than the giver expected. God's providence has often done what God's servant here foreshadows. Through many a season of deep distress has the Church of God passed, when the sons of the prophets have been threatened with famine. And the records of God's dealings with them, to supply their wants and to shield them from threatening harm, are as truly wonderful and as truly evidences of divine guardianship as the miracles here recorded of Elisha. The significance of these wonders should be noticed; and we should acknowledge that like marvels belong to the constant dealings of God, who is the Author both of Scripture and of providence.

The significancy of the next wonder recorded of this prophet is of sufficient interest to bid us delay for its deliberate consideration. The narrative might suggest some profitable thoughts incidentally, from which we select only this one to stop for a moment the onward flow of our direct mediations. See upon what feeble instrumentalities the important events of a man's history may be made to turn! A little maid, waiting upon Naaman's wife, says, "Would God my Lord were with the prophet!" But for these words from a mouth of a child, Naaman had still remained a leper and an idolater! Yet indeed a long train of providences had prepared the way for these words. Little things of great power do not stand alone. War with Israel had preceded; prisoners had been carried captive; a pious household had been invaded; a child had been carried off to the dismay of weeping parents; that child had been carefully taught in her early years, and while yet a little maid in a land of paganism forgot not Samaria's prophet. In a household of distress she forgot her own captivity to sympathize with the family in which her unhappy lot was cast. Her cheering words were repeated in the ears of the miserable, and they opened the only door of hope. How many blessings would come to us all if we were more careful to note and improve the minor providences of life! Who is too feeble to do a great good, since a little Hebrew maid may lead a Syrian nobleman to the faith of her people? Who should not watch for opportunities to tell leprous souls of the great Prophet who can cure worse maladies than those of the body? Who of those that are more deeply diseased than the general of Syria's armies—with a malady that earth cannot cure—should not gladly hear of those healing waters in which none have ever bathed in vain? Let who will speak of these things in their ears—though a little maid, though in familiar teachings—let the leper gladly hear the message, "Go, wash and be clean."

For Naaman's necessities are significant, and the world is filled with just such as he.

We speak not of his station in society. He was a great man with his master, and his master was king of the land. He was the general of Syria's armies. He was honorable and highly esteemed. Wealth was his; servants did his bidding; honours were heaped upon him. But these are small matters, even in the world's esteem. Men court them, yet they know well that the vilest often possess them, and the worthy of the land are held in low regard; they know that the highest often fall very low upon any turn of fortune; they know that the noblest must soon be crowded out of sight by their successors. Naaman was a great man. If he deserved his honours, well. But whether he deserved them or not, they soon left him; and while he had them they were marred by a serious want. And if a man's honours are all of earth, they are seriously lacking; and thus we may write of every one, He is a great man, BUT— Perhaps if we knew just what thing troubles those who occupy the high places around us, we would not exchange with those we are now disposed to envy. Some people keep their troubles more concealed than Naaman could his. Poor man! with all his honours he was a leper!

We do not speak of his race. He was not a Hebrew, but a Syrian. Naturally he would have little to do with Israel's prophet, and the prophet little to do with him. They were thrown into separate associations; so that it seemed a chance—if the world, which is made and filled with the presence of one Infinite God, has any room where a chance can be crowded in—that the leper heard at all of the healer. Elisha, like his Master of later times, was not sent but to the lost sheep of the house of Israel; yet as Elijah blessed the Sidonian widow, and as Christ gave some goodly crumbs from his table to feed the Gentile poor, so there are foreshadowings of gospel grace in Elisha's dealings with the Syrian. And if here are lessons of the divine sovereignty—as our Lord declares—that so many in Israel remain defiled while Naaman is cleansed, yet the Great Teacher will not allow us to forget that this is to the great reproach of those who withhold due honour from the prophets by whom they too might find cleansing.

The chief thing to claim our notice respecting Naaman is his disease. He was a leper. In all the Scriptures, in the teachings of Moses, and not less in the teachings of Christ, the leprosy seems to be set forth not simply as a disease natural, but specially as a disease typical. It is representative of the great disease hereditary in the race of man since the great apostasy of the garden of Eden:

"Sin like a venomous disease,
Infects our vital blood."

Everywhere in the Bible is the leprosy spoken of as an unclean disease; we do not certainly know that it was contagious; and the rule for separating lepers from the society of others was not always strictly observed. Here we find Naaman still associating with others, though a leper; a little later in the same book we find other lepers having some intercourse with society. Yet the law of Moses is very explicit in forbidding clean persons to associate with lepers: "The leper in whom the plague is, his clothes shall be rent and his head bare, and he shall put a covering upon his upper lip, and shall cry Unclean, unclean. All the days wherein the plague shall be in him he shall be defiled; he is unclean; he shall dwell alone; without the camp shall his habitation be." Lev. xiii. 45, 46. How unhappy was the estate of a leprous man when these laws were strictly enforced!

"Depart, depart, O child
Of Israel, from the temple of thy God!
For he hath smote thee with his chastening rod,
And to the desert wild,
From all thou lovest, away thy feet must flee,
That from thy plague his people may be free."

Even the parents, the wife or children of a leper dare not approach him after the priest had pronounced him diseased. In fact he became as a dead man to all around him, and every regulation was significant of this. He was unclean, and his touch, like that of a dead body, polluted everything. He must rend his garments, as if he was a mourner at his own funeral. The bare head and the covered lip and the loud cry were tokens of mourning. So when the prophet Ezekiel was forbidden to mourn, he was told not to do the very things required of the lepers: "Forbear to cry, make no mourning for the dead, bind the tire of thine head upon thee, ... and cover not thy lips." Ezek. xxiv. 17. In restoring a leper the very same ceremonies of cleansing by cedar wood, hyssop and scarlet that belonged elsewhere only in matters pertaining to death were always employed. The Jewish law made the leper worse than an outcast. He was as a dead man. He must live without the camp; when he tasted water it must be from the stagnant pool, and not from a running stream, lest some clean person farther down the banks might taste the same water. When any one approached, he must raise his doleful cry and let them know that he was unclean. When the leprosy passed over into Europe with the returning tides of men from the Crusades—though, indeed, it made its appearance as early as the sixth century, after the decline of the Roman empire—it prevailed to a fearful extent, and the sanitary regulations respecting it were excessively severe. Legally and politically, the leper was reckoned a dead man. The marriage vow was cancelled, and his wife was as a widow, allowed to marry again if she chose; his estate passed to his heirs; the very ceremonies of burial were performed for him, and masses were said for the repose of his soul. Better for any man to be dead than to be leprous. Death is a less terrible form of bereavement than for a beloved one to be thus an outcast; and the victim had not the quiet of the grave, though earth had no hopes for him.

Leprosy is the great scriptural type of sin. The Jews regarded its infliction as a direct judgment of God; and the cases of Miriam, Num. xii. 12, and Gehazi, 2 Kings v. 27, and Uzziah, 2 Chron. xxvi. 19, 20, as recorded in the Scriptures, support this view. No art of man could cure it. So the king of Israel exclaims here (2 Kings v. 7): "Am I God, to kill and make alive, that this man doth send unto me to recover a man of his leprosy?" Therefore every regulation implied that as recovery could be expected only from divine power, the leper was sent not to the physicians, but to the priests, and the ceremonies of the recovered leper were acts of thanksgiving to God.

It does not appear that regulations so strict belonged to the tribes around, or were always maintained in Israel. Naaman may not have been placed in the distressing circumstance of a leprous Jew. But he was a leper, and he gladly heard tidings of healing. That he put any credit in the thought of healing may strike us as strange. Look at the conduct of the several persons named in the narrative. We have no account that ever a leper was healed in Israel from the days of Miriam to the days of Elisha. We may admire the trusting and childlike faith of the little Hebrew girl, who lifted up her voice in the darkness of Syria to speak of her country's prophet and to wish that her lord was with him in Samaria. We may contrast her with her own idolatrous king, who never thought of Elisha when Naaman asked the healing of his disease. We may judge that Naaman acted wisely when he made his immediate preparations to seek the prophet, though doubtless despair of relief from any other quarter was his chief impelling motive. Could a man afflicted with the leprosy be given up by all ordinary physicians, and be unwilling at any effort or cost to try any means that held forth the slightest hope that relief might come, and that the current of health would flow vigorously through his veins?

But from considering Naaman's sad and significant condition, we may pass to speak of the means he used to seek relief, and the steps he was willing to take to secure it. Not those whose condition is worst, not those who have the readiest access to relief, either long most wistfully or seek most earnestly for a cure. "Many lepers were in Israel in the days of Elisha;" the fame of his miracles had filled the land, yet though he had raised the dead, no outcast drew near the wondrous prophet. But a Syrian idolater presses past them all to find the cleansings of Jordan. Yet Naaman began his journey all unready for a cure. He came with a letter from a king to a king, and all the parties were ignorant of the important matter they had then in hand. He came with the swelling pride of a Syrian and a prince, for indeed he had two diseases, and the grace of Israel's God was larger than Naaman's thoughts, and designed to heal him of both. First he brought his letter to Jehoram, and the Israelitish king thought it but the pretext for war between the two nations. At this juncture Elisha proffered his services. It requires no little wisdom for the prophet to discern when he should seek opportunities for doing good, and when those who desire good must seek him. No general rule can decide in such matters. Elisha was truly concerned for the honour of religion, and such a spirit best prepares us to use our occasions of doing good judiciously. Perhaps Naaman's pride was flattered and his expectations raised by the prophet's voluntary message calling him to receive his cure.

But his expectations were disappointed. No sooner did the splendid equipage stand at the prophet's door than, without giving him time to bring forward the presents which according to Oriental etiquette belong to the opening of such an interview, he was met by a messenger from the prophet, who bade him go and wash in Jordan seven times, and his flesh should come again to him and he should be clean. Such a message and so delivered filled the haughty Syrian with rage. He knew something, and this seemed opposed to all he knew. He had his prejudices, and this cut across them all. He had formed his anticipations of how the prophet would do this great thing, and this dealing was all unlike them. As to washing in water to heal the leprosy, had he not often bathed himself and remained a leper as before? As to any special efficacy in the Jordan, why was it superior to the golden stream Abana and the cool, pure waters of the Pharpar in his own city? Why did not the prophet come out himself? Why did he not do something that would seem to possess the power to effect this needed cure? Rage possessed the leper's heart. He ordered his chariot-driver to turn away from the prophet's door; his anger perhaps kept him just then from realizing the disappointment, and he thought himself a fool to come so far upon a fruitless errand.

And so Naaman nearly missed a cure. Let him indulge this rage and refuse the Jordan, and he may remain a leper—he may remain a heathen still. And indeed it was a very simple thing which the prophet bade him do. Naaman had long been familiar with the disease; a modern missionary says that the leprosy still cleaves to Damascus and is still incurable.* How could he consent to so simple a cure as this? But truly its very simplicity was a

* The Land and the Book, ii. 199, 519.

sufficient reason why Naaman should not leave this method of cure untried. So, with true and respectful faithfulness, his servants urged him to this. They knew that so great was his anxiety for a cure that he would willingly endure severe trials, pay large sums of money and return the largest gratitude to his benefactor. How ready, then, should he be to do this easy thing! "My father!" they asked with affectionate tenderness and unanswerable logic, "if the prophet had bidden thee do some great thing, wouldst thou not have done it? How much rather then, when he saith to thee, wash and be clean!" How indebted was Naaman to his servants! His wife's little maid-servant sent him to Samaria—his attendants there prevented him from going home unhealed. He went down to the Jordan—a distance of perhaps twenty-five miles—bathed seven times in its waters, and was cleansed.

So Naaman was no more a leper. What a changed sight in the eyes of his servants, when he came forth from the healing stream with the ruddy glow of health instead of the ghastly paleness—with the upright form and the cheerful eye and the firm step which they had never expected to see again! What a changed feeling in the man himself from these invigorating waters! How hard to realize the effect of this sudden restoration! Not only that the sluggish blood now moves rapidly though the veins, nor that the skin and flesh are sound, but the dull despair of incurable calamity no longer binds the heartstrings. Health and life are his again: he may go forth freely among his fellows, and it seems not only a new lease of time, but a new world in which to live, a new zeal for every duty, a new enjoyment for every pleasure.

There are more lepers in the world than Naaman, and worse cases by far of leprosy. There are others besides him offended at the simplicity of the divine means of care, and many indeed who turn utterly away and are never healed. There are two long chapters in the books of Moses (see Lev. xiii., xiv.) that describe such a leprosy as belonged to this Syrian general, only the particulars are so many and so beyond a parallel to any disease existing in the world, affecting clothes and houses and even fretting and consuming the very stones, that it seems expressly adapted to serve as a typical disease. And though, as we have noticed, no instance of cure is recorded after Miriam until Naaman, yet the very provisions of the law seem to imply that healing was possible—to teach that sometimes it was cured, and to hold forth some hope to the suffering. Yet many lepers were in Israel—we soon after read of four in this very city—and none of them applied to the prophet for a cure until Naaman, or indeed after Naaman. But we can see in Christian lands more remarkable apathy than this.

Not two chapters of the Bible only, but the whole book from Genesis to Revelation, is chiefly occupied in describing a more fearful leprosy, and in declaring the only, the free, the efficacious, remedy for it. How sin pollutes the soul, how it separates man from man and the race from God, how it makes its subject outlaws from his government, incapacitates from the services and enjoyments of his holy creatures, and puts them among the spiritually dead that are banished from his sight,—all this it tells. Yet many lepers have been healed. The law of grace not only makes provision for cleansing, but, better far than the law of Moses, it invites the leprous to be cleansed. And as Elisha sent Naaman to the Jordan, so this fearful leprosy is cleansed by purifying waters. There is a Fountain opened for sin and for uncleanness, and it is not here, as in Israel, that we cannot point to cases of its purifying power. Many have been healed, and their happy experience may encourage others to come as they came, that they too may find a cure. And as the prophet offered to heal Naaman, so a cure is offered to sinful souls. There is no excuse for the unbelief by which so many are for ever ruined. These sacred pages describe in the plainest terms the fearful malady, tell that the sinner is dead to holiness and dead to God, and declare that there is no remedy elsewhere than in Christ Jesus. So also they call the leper to find healing. As when our Lord was upon the earth no leper asked his cleansing power and departed from his presence still a leper, so now stands he ready to heal all who seek his grace; and to every unhealed soul he declares as truly as to the men around him then, "Ye will not come unto me that ye might have life."

In Naaman we see an example similar to the thoughts of many. How many there are who in their secret minds often wish they were Christians —often say they would be willing to do anything if they might but find the salvation of the gospel, and often bewail their own sad condition that they know not how to come to Christ for life! They think they are willing to return to God, if they only had the opportunity. And they are doubtless willing, in the same sense that Naaman was willing to come to Samaria, willing to submit to mysterious things, willing to pay any money; but they are not willing to do the simple matter which the gospel requires. They are therefore ready to find fault with the things that are required, and to do the things that are of no use. The simplicity of the gospel offends them. The false religions of the world prove that men are ready to do some great things to make amends for sin. They will be pilgrims and self-torturers; they will endure fastings and penances; they will give lands and moneys; they will go through with services that seem to mean something; they want to feel the oppressive burden of sin, and to find self-righteous satisfaction in keen pangs of anguish. How many are the great things men are ready to do, as the false prophets of the earth humour the fantasies of the sin-sick soul, and vainly tell them that thus they may secure the pardon of their sins and the healing of their deep-seated malady!

Naaman was a great man with his master, but how unhappy had he been if then he had been disobedient! There was nothing for him to do but to receive the prophet's word and to bathe in the Jordan. And there is nothing effectual the sinful soul can do but to come to Christ. This is not so much *coming up* to the requirements of the gospel as it is *coming down* to them. The very simplicity of the divine requirement is the sinner's stumbling-block. He has his thought of how the thing is to be done, and he is ready to take offence, even though he risks the loss of his soul, at anything that falls not in with his preconceived opinions. He has heard of the experience by which others have come to Christ, and unless he passes their way he judges he cannot come at all. Men limit the teachings of the Spirit, and consent not to be guided by him in the ways of his choosing. Let the case of Naaman suggest to us what doubtless is true—that no man ever comes to Christ without being disappointed as to his own anticipations—perhaps bitterly disappointed—and this by divine wisdom and mercy, for the very purpose of staining the pride of human glory and of leading us to give the honour of our salvation where it belongs—to God. Let us read that declaration of Isaiah, applicable to his people in all ages: "I will bring the blind by a way that they know not; I will lead them in paths that they have not known," Isa. xlii. 16.

But what matter to Naaman if his thoughts were disappointed, his prejudices overthrown and his pride mortified, when yet his leprosy was cleansed? That was the great thing after all, and he was ready to leap for joy and to vow all his sacrifices hereafter only to the Lord God of Israel. So let every leper give up his thoughts and submit to the divine method of mercy. You that are so ready to promise such great things to secure salvation, how much more should you be prepared to take the offered grace of Christ in all its freeness! You have long been trying to see your way before you, and are not willing to take step by step the path of his leadings. You have been long wondering how you can cleanse yourselves—how you can fit yourselves for the requirements of the gospel—how you can prepare yourselves to come to Christ. You have looked for an experience full of mystery—some more powerful preaching than you have ever heard before—some great working of a strange and indisputable power. If you could have some extraordinary feelings—something that is beyond question the working of the Spirit's grace—you would be well satisfied. The gospel is too simple for you. Yet thus God works. He converts men by means as unlikely as Naaman's washing in the Jordan. Thousands of men have been converted under very ordinary sermons; the simpler the preaching is, so that it be God's truth, the more is he honoured. What you want is to come to Christ, and it matters not how simple are the means that lead you there. The voice of a child sent Naaman from Syria; the words of the prophet offended him; the expostulations of his servants led him to the Jordan, and obedient faith secured his cleansing. Foolish men sometimes go indignantly away from the sanctuary, where they have been taught disappointing things. Yet this is their folly. How much more should they do what God demands that they may be saved!

Abana and Pharpar were not better than the Jordan. Naaman might have washed all his life in Syria's waters, and been a leper still. And the leprosy of sin can only be washed away in the blood of Jesus. Vain are all resources till the soul comes to him. And how must the sinner come? Without delay, without preparation and without doubt. What preparation needs the sick man for his physician except his sickness; the beggar for his benefactor but his poverty; the leper for cleansing but his leprosy! Naaman could not prepare for healing; Naaman's rank and gifts were of no esteem in the prophet's eyes; Naaman was a leper and needed Jordan's cleansing stream. There are various degrees of sinfulness among guilty men; but for this one great reason need they all a Saviour—that they are sinners, and for help must they come to him. But, alas! the story of Naaman, over and over again—the same pride, the same expectation of something great—meets us in every age. But pride disguises itself under humble expressions. "I am so great a sinner; I have so hard a heart; I am too unworthy; there is nothing good in me." Yet this is all false humility. It is Naaman over again. Do you mean that you could trust Christ to save a better heart, but you cannot expect him to bless so hard a heart? If you were better you would come, but you cannot as you are? So, foolish sinner, you want to bring a price in your hands. One of your dignity cannot be received like other sinners. Does it become a leper to make such terms? Come to be forgiven; come to be cleansed; come to take Christ at his word when he declares, "Him that cometh unto me I will in nowise cast out." As Naaman's sole warrant was the bidding of the prophet, so let any and every guilty sinner obey the word of Christ and COME.

CHAPTER X.

THE HEALING WATERS OF ISRAEL.

IT startles us to think how nearly Naaman's pride prevailed toward keeping him still a leper. Though he knew well the wretchedness of his disease, and would have bought its cure at any price, his pride refuses to stoop, and his blind and foolish rage had nearly sent him back to a life of incurable misery. The question is easily answered if we ask, "Whose would have been the loss if the Syrian general had gone home unhealed?" Attribute any possible motive to Elisha; suppose that he had not treated Naaman's case judiciously, and that the failure of a cure had grieved the prophet for his own unfaithfulness in duty; or suppose that his judicious and well-meant kindness had not reached its aim through Naaman's ignorant and proud folly, and that thus Elisha was grieved without any reason to blame himself; still, it must be seen that Naaman himself must bear the chief consequences of the serious truth that he is still a leper. Yet all this is chiefly valuable now for the warnings it holds forth to sinful men. Still those who draw near the prophets of God, as Naaman came to Elisha, are prone to take offence at the manner or the messages of those who preach the gospel. This offence may be more or less like Naaman's. There may be a rage expressed in words, or there may simply be an undefined disappointment, distaste and indifference to the biddings of the preacher; there may be a decided preference for some other method of pleasing God, aside from the simple requirements of the gospel, as Naaman preferred the waters of Damascus to the Jordan; or there may be simply the neglect of the prescribed washing in the opened and purifying Fountain! Or indeed the offence may have a better foundation upon which to rest than the rage of Naaman. Not every servant of God is as wise in his measures or as truthful in his words as Elisha. The minister may have given to his hearer *some* just ground of offence. He may have spoken unkindly, or at least not with the full sympathy of his great Master; he may have so misunderstood the case as to give injudicious directions; he may have been unfaithful to the true teachings of the gospel: make the most possible case you can of it, and yet, in the light of Naaman's leprosy, see how dangerous it is for any man to take offence at the gospel or to turn away from Christ. A man is justified for turning away from a false or unfaithful prophet, just as he would from an ignorant or unskilful physician, but if he wishes to be healed he must turn to the true and the faithful: all quarreling with truth, for any possible reason, is unwise, and cannot result to any man's advantage. What it becomes us especially to notice is, that no man can safely take offence at religion because of any religious doctrines, or because of the manners or doings of any religious teachers, so as to continue himself in indifference or irreligion. Reject human additions, but beware of neglecting God's word; care little for man, but venture not to reject Christ. Let the reasons be what they may, pride, ignorance and folly are at the bottom of all such rejections, and the loss of the soul is the inevitable result.

If Naaman had rejected the counsel of Elisha, he might have been able to satisfy the people of Syria that he was right, that he showed only a praiseworthy spirit, and that the Israelitish prophet was but an impostor; but it would be true still that he had turned away from the only means of healing, that his pride had ruined all his subsequent life, and that he was yet a leper. And if any sinner under the sound of the gospel takes such offence at anything he sees or hears or imagines in the Church, or touching its officers or members, that he remains impenitent in his sins or unbelieving toward Christ, this result, no matter what its source, is reached to his own undoing. We are ready to acknowledge and bewail there are evils in the Church, which we do not attempt to justify. False doctrines are taught, injudicious directions are given to inquiring sinners, an improper spirit is often exhibited where we expect something better.

We make no apology for these things. They are not peculiar to religion; they are not confined to our times: the great Head of the Church, when he set up his kingdom among sinful men, did not design to admit only pure and infallible men; on the contrary, he declared that the wheat and the tares would both grow together in the same field. There are things to take just offence at in a Church that has evils in it; yet if the Church spoke only the truth, and in a proper spirit, proud men would often turn away in a rage, as Naaman was offended at the words of Elisha. And it pertains to every thoughtful man to notice that the burden of mischief done falls upon the man who, for any reason, turns away from Christ and salvation. What Naaman needed was a cure; whatever hindered that left him still diseased. Had he gone to a prophet who could not cure, or turned away in his foolish rage from one that could, had his servants fostered his pride or kept silent, the end would have been the same. The man who does not find the sinner's only Saviour, no matter what kept him away, must remain a sinner and meet a sinner's doom. How great therefore is their folly who take any offence at the doctrines or the leadings of piety, and refuse to bathe in the great Fountain! We cannot afford to take offence at Jesus and his cross. We who are so defiled with the leprosy of sin must draw near to Jesus and say, Lord, if thou wilt thou canst make me clean!

Naaman returned from the Jordan cleansed, thankful and filled with new purposes of service to be rendered to the God of Israel. He stood again with his company before the prophet's door, and would gladly have left with him substantial gifts in token of his gratitude. The prophet absolutely declined to receive any. In Eastern lands the exchange of presents is much more common than with us; to refuse them is indeed an incivility, if not worse; but Naaman is quite changed since his bathing in the Jordan: he is little disposed now to judge unkindly of anything done by the prophet; he cannot question that his course is quite disinterested; and perhaps, indeed, Oriental etiquette demanded that the gifts upon his part should have been the first step of their intercourse. Elisha had skilfully avoided this by his message before the Syrian could enter his door; and Naaman's hasty rage may have lasted long enough to bear him some distance from the city on his way toward Damascus before his servants could prevail upon him to do as the prophet bade. So now, indeed, even etiquette gives the Syrian no room to complain. Why the prophet refused to receive anything we are not told. It is usually said that Elisha was zealous for the honour of Israel's God, and desired to show this newly-converted idolater that the servants of Jehovah were not mercenary, as the priests of all false religions notoriously are. Yet what afterward occurred shows plainly that Elisha did not suffer himself to be much concerned even for injurious impressions that were falsely made upon the mind of Naaman. When Gehazi told falsehoods in the prophet's name, and received from the Syrian, as if Elisha had sent him, the very gifts now refused, we have no record that any attempt was made to disabuse the mind of Naaman touching this matter. It would seem far more indelicate for Elisha to send after the gifts, upon any plea, than to receive them as offered at the first; yet the Syrian was allowed to go home under the impression that this was done by the prophet's order.

It is difficult for a servant of God to know just what steps to take to vindicate his reputation when slanderous reports are made of him. Sometimes silence is a confession of guilt, and duty requires a man to speak. At other times it is far best to take no notice whatever of current falsehoods. They will die of themselves if let alone, or Providence will sufficiently refute them without our concerning ourselves with them, or the general tenour of a holy life will forbid people to believe them, or even those who have set them in circulation become ashamed of them and give the lie to them by the esteem in which they are compelled to hold the subject of their slanders. Those who are much concerned about what other people say or do touching them, have profitless work to attend to, which will likely grow upon their hands while pleasanter and better duties are neglected. Elisha knew that

Gehazi had used his name in falsehood and robbery with Naaman, but this was not his fault, and he made it little his concern.

When Elisha will not receive the gifts of the grateful Syrian, Naaman becomes his petitioner. He boldly avows his faith in the God of Israel. There were many of Elisha's own nation at that hour who observed a mixed worship, paying some reverence to Jehovah while also they served Jeroboam's golden calves. But Naaman perceives at once that the God who could heal his leprosy by means so simple was the one living God. This God alone was worthy of his love and service, nor would he offer sacrifices hereafter to any but to him. But we naturally judge that the new-born zeal of Naaman, however sincere, was uninstructed. The converting grace of God works moral rather than natural changes upon the soul. Naaman was an Israelite in mind and temper by turning to the God of Israel, but the change into the intelligent and full knowledge of the teachings of Israel could not so suddenly come. He seems here to fall into two errors, both of which the prophet deals kindly by: *First,* he asks that he may be allowed to take with him some of the earth of Judea, for henceforth he would offer sacrifices only to Jehovah. Evidently some religious purpose was intended by this, upon which he sought the prophet's approval, for without this he could easily have taken the earth away unasked. Whether he designed to build an altar of the earth, or to kneel upon this sacred soil as he offered his devotions, or for some other of the various purposes suggested by different commentators, is a matter we need not discuss. *Next*, he asks a harder thing—that he may be forgiven for conforming to the usual ceremonies which belonged to his position in the court of the king of Syria, and which he himself felt to be an undue compliance with the idolatries in which now he could bear no part. We cannot think that Naaman asks, as Lightfoot suggests, to be forgiven for his past idolatry, for he need not speak of this as connected with service to the king, since he had been an idolater all his life, both in and out of office. But he speaks as if his civil duties demanded an external compliance with idolatrous services, and he asked to be pardoned for this upon the plea that his heart was not in them.

The important question is, in reference to these matters, when Elisha said to Naaman, Go in peace, did he give his approbation, as a prophet of God, to the request of the Syrian?—especially did he imply that he would be justified in compliances with idolatrous practices because his king demanded it?

In considering this, we are not so much surprised at the request of Naaman. He had been all his life an idolater, and was but a child in his knowledge of the teachings of true religion. Yet we must give him credit in the main matter here spoken of for a correct discernment of the consistent duty of a worshipper of Israel's God. Naaman's own conscience decides that bowing in the temple of Syrian idolatry was not in harmony with a professed subjection to the only true God. And innumerable teachings in the Scripture support this decision. If Naaman could bow in the house of Rimmon because his king bade, why did the three young friends of Daniel refuse so steadfastly to bow before the golden image on the plain of Dura at the command of Nebuchadnezzar? We are quite unwilling, then, to understand that there is any approval on the part of the prophet of this proposal, and indeed no definite reply of Elisha is recorded to either of Naaman's requests. That the prophet dismissed him with the ordinary courtesy, Go in peace—which is but equivalent to our "farewell"—cannot be interpreted to favour a sentiment otherwise unscriptural. The design of the record is not to solve a question in casuistry which is elsewhere abundantly and plainly solved in the sacred writings, but rather to show us how quickly such questions rise in a mind that is truly awakened to see the just and holy claims of the living God. Some indeed suppose that Elisha saw such evident proofs of true piety in Naaman, but struggling with the misconceptions natural to a mind so long accustomed to paganism, that he was willing to dismiss him without any direct answer, and to allow him to solve the question for himself under the guidance of the Holy Spirit. And there is doubtless a great deal of forbearance due to young converts to true piety, whose previous life unfits them for an immediate recognition of all the claims of the gospel : there is a harmony and coherency in all the great teachings of true religion, so that a humble, devout and sincere mind will soon work loose from early errors and misconceptions; there is wisdom in allowing a thoughtful mind to discover for itself the path of duty, rather than to make it dependent on others to have every step pointed out; and there is an earnest tenderness of conscience in Naaman, which the prophet judges may be allowed to make its own decisions.

Now, when we add that there is no proof that Naaman ever did bow himself down after this in this house of Rimmon, but when rather the likelihood seems all the other way, it appears unjust to Elisha to gather from this narrative that he approved of his proposal to do this thing. Naaman disappears from the history from this time on. We read soon again of Syria and of Syrian wars with Israel, but this officer of the king, this great man with his master, this general of their armies, is heard of no more. So far as his health was concerned, he was better fit for his place than ever. Naaman was no more a leper. But when he bathed in the Jordan he got a better cure than the king of Syria intended. Naaman was no more an idolater, and doubtless his new ideas did not find favour in the palaces of Damascus. In a very little time afterward we read that Hazael is the captain of the king's host. We may reflect that Benhadad gained but little when he displaced a man who was conscientious to disobey his God, and put in his room another who did not scruple to murder his king. The tendency of the entire history may warrant us in judging that Naaman easily decided this question of duty, and that he soon lost his honours for the sake of his religion; for in all ages the substantial claims of God upon his people remain the same. When we take up our cross and follow Jesus, we are but copying the examples set before us in all the history of the Church. Abraham left his father's house; Moses gave up the honours of Egypt; Naaman probably lost his place in the court of Syria; none of these perhaps without a struggle, but all really decided in the hour of trial. And whosoever now is not ready to forsake all at the bidding of Christ cannot be his disciple. We may follow him with tearful eyes, but we must follow him or we are not worthy of him.

CHAPTER XI.

GEHAZI'S GUILT AND PUNISHMENT.

BUT let us now turn to consider another character hitherto brought rather to our favourable notice. Herodotus records for us an elaborate address of Solon to Crœsus, the moral of which is, Call no man happy until the day of his death, for we know not what miserable changes may yet lie before a living man. Up to this time Gehazi may have maintained a fair reputation as the servant of the prophet. He was, it may be, under the prophet's instructions, as Elisha had himself been the servant of Elijah. But now he falls sadly under the power of a temptation which presented a fair opportunity of securing wealth and at but little risk of discovery. Elisha has sent Naaman away, refusing his gifts. It is not likely he will ever see his face again. Now Gehazi thinks this is the time for him. If he can but secure these presents despised by his master, how happy it would make him! Elisha will never know the matter. Naaman is rich enough to give what Gehazi asks without missing it, and generous enough to feel gratified rather than robbed by this disposal of his wealth.

So Gehazi allowed the Syrian to depart only far enough to enable him still to reach him before he was quite gone, while he escaped the prophet's notice and planned the plausible story which would sufficiently account to Naaman for the change in Elisha's mind. So Gehazi ran after the chariot of the Syrian. The attendants saw a man running behind and wishing to attract their attention: he was soon recognized as the prophet's servant, and Naaman himself, with every mark of respect, alighted from his chariot to salute him. Doubtless the sons of the prophets were a care upon Elisha, not only for instruction but for support; and this forms the foundation for Gehazi's plea. It is well that he had a generous and unsuspicious man to deal with, or his claim would have betrayed itself. A talent of silver is variously estimated at from fifteen hundred to two thousand dollars. Such a sum of money would scarcely be found in the possession of a student of divinity in the poverty-stricken schools of Elisha. They who enlarge their buildings by their own labours and by borrowed tools, as we read in the next chapter, are content with humbler aspirations. But Gehazi has not miscalculated upon the penetration of Naaman in these matters, nor upon his generosity in giving freely at his request. Rather he urges double as much upon him. Gehazi is more successful than he had expected. The grateful Syrian, not content with giving double, sends his servants to carry the gifts for him. Perhaps Gehazi would willingly have dispensed with their attendance, which might be noticed and might bring the whole transaction to the knowledge of Elisha. But he did not dare to decline the dangerous kindness, lest he should betray himself. All succeeded, however, as well as Gehazi could expect. The treasure was safely deposited in a secret place, the servants of Naaman were dismissed, the stately train passed on to Damascus; no man in Samaria knew Gehazi's deception, and the servant, all innocent to appearence, stood before the prophet.

Thus it often is in the ways of sin. Men lay their plans to escape detection; their early efforts seem quite successful, and they flatter themselves with thoughts of their own wisdom. Gehazi's sins were—

(1.) Covetousness. He heard the offer of the grateful Syrian and Elisha's refusal, and he longed to make himself master of that which was not his. Perhaps indeed he deceived himself with the reflection that he asked only a small portion of what the Syrian had freely offered. Naaman had brought with him ten talents of silver and six thousand pieces of gold—perhaps equal to seventy thousand dollars. In the eyes of Gehazi a very small part of this was a fortune. The Scriptures warn us that we have to do with scarcely any more deceitful thing than the love of money. The amount of money a man desires differs with his previous experience, just as wealth is a comparative term.

Let every man guard the avenues of his heart against admitting that most dangerous foe to peace and innocence—the love of money. Andrew Fuller remarks that three classes of persons are specially in danger of covetousness: *prosperous men,* because the habit of acquiring is apt to strengthen the desire for it; *aged persons,* because the decay of the natural powers may change a man's taste in other directions, while he is able as ever to make and enjoy money; and *professors of religion,* because such men are restrained from gross external sins by a regard to their own consistency, while they may feel free to indulge secret tendencies which bring little reproach upon them in the eyes of men. A man may be covetous while he does nothing to defraud others.

(2.) Theft belonged to Gehazi's sin. A man may be covetous when he is not dishonest, but Gehazi is both. It does not relieve the matter any that Naaman freely gave the money into his hands, that he did not miss it from his wealth, or that he pressed more upon him than he asked; for Gehazi well knew that the money was given for no such purpose as he received it. He took what in no proper sense belonged to him; all the pretences that would make this any less than robbery were frivolous and false; Gehazi had all the guilt of a robber without the boldness that theft sometimes requires. There are different modes of robbery. By forgery and gaming and fraudulent pretences, and in our prices and payments of money worth less than the amount at which it is honourably reckoned when the giver and the receiver both knew its value, men take from others what they ought not to get; and all these frauds are breaches of that precept of Sinai which declares, "Thou shalt not steal."

(3.) Gehazi spoke falsehoods. Not only once but repeatedly he uttered lying words. His story to Naaman was totally false; his answer to Elisha as much so. Nothing has truly a higher importance among men than truth. Yet men speak falsehood abundantly. Many who are indignant when they are imposed upon by others, themselves use the lying tongue. Many are not careful to speak the truth in small matters. Rather than defer a slight inconvenience, they indulge in lying. It is a degrading and wicked habit. The prophet's servant speaks falsehoods so easily and with so little concern that we are tempted to think it is no new thing with him. God abhors falsehood, and declares that the mouth of them that speak lies shall be stopped.

(4.) Gehazi was hypocritical. We see this in his appearance before Elisha. He came into the house in an unconcerned and indifferent manner, designing to conceal the fact of his absence at all; and when questioned upon the subject did not hesitate to declare that he had gone nowhere. And if he was one of the sons of the prophets, if the money of Naaman turned him away from the frugal fare and the hard service to which Elisha had devoted his life, then here is a sad shipwreck of his professed faith.

The sin of Gehazi was great, and his enjoyment of his ill-gotten stores was soon marred. Elisha calmly asked him whence he came; and upon his false reply, he showed him not only that he knew his sin, but also that he was well aware of his secret plans for the future. Visions of wealth filled Gehazi's mind. Money and garments were already his; oliveyards, vineyards, cattle and servants were in the landscape his imagination had already drawn for the years to come. How terrible the prophet's words! Let sinners hear and tremble. These are some of the lessons: 1st. Every man's sin is known. Man may not know of it. You may speak hypocritical falsehoods before a servant of God, and he neither know nor rebuke it. But God knows always. There is no such thing as a secret sin. There are witnesses who will tell. Conscience will tell; angels and devils will tell; God will bring everything out to the light. Many a sin may be more skilfully planned and longer hid than Gehazi's. But every sin is known. 2d. Every sin will receive due punishment. God often brings upon men just such punishments as seem fitting for their offence; and in what they suffer they cannot but see what brought their wretchedness upon them. Gehazi in his leprosy could never forget

Naaman. And this was worse than his; for the Syrian's disease was a calamity, and this was a judgment. 3d. His punishment was public. He did this thing secretly, and thought it would never be known. But God brought it out before Israel and before the sun. Wherever Gehazi went, men discerned the proof of his sin and of divine justice. He was widely known as the prophet's servant; and still wherever he went in all Israel he must be a preacher of the divine law. No man could see Gehazi without recalling Naaman's story and thus learning of God's cleansing grace; yet this man himself was a solemn warning that God is just. And examples enough, both to warn and to encourage, occur all around us. It is true many seem to sin with impunity. Some sins God punishes plainly here, lest men should deny his justice; yet he does not punish every sin here, lest men should think there is no hereafter. Enough to warn the wicked, enough to encourage the penitent we may see on every hand. 4th. Gehazi's punishment affected more than himself. It came upon his seed after him. The leprosy is hereditary. Children seem to be free from it, but it is in the system, and will make its fearful appearance sooner or later. And so we know it is with men's sin. We are social beings, and we cannot sin alone. God indeed shows mercy to the children of wicked men when they love him and keep his commandments; but we know that men cannot sin and bear the fearful crime alone. The character, prospects, prosperity, health and reputation of a family are deeply involved in what the parent is, and in what he says and does. No man can possibly know what is before him when he consents to any sin. He knows not what strange circumstance which he has overlooked may awaken inquiry and lead to his detection. He cannot tell who may yet be involved with him in the punishment which he must bear. Let us remember that sin is against God; that he has made nothing in the universe capable of resisting his will; and that he can make everything about us, and our own consciences within us, testify to the divine supremacy and the divine justice in punishing sin.

In this whole record pertaining to Gehazi the most serious lesson is that which reminds us that men possessed of the best religious opportunities may still be rebels against God and may fall beneath the divine wrath. When we read of this Syrian leper healed by Israel's waters and avowing his faithful service to the God of Jacob, our hearts rejoice over him as a trophy of redeeming grace. But when in the same chapter we read that Elisha's trusted servant, who had enjoyed the teachings and example of such a prophet, falls so low as this, we have a sad lesson of human iniquity. Education is not religion, however valuable its services are to instruct men in the fear of the Lord. Our families may be taught the great things of the kingdom of

God, but it is by no means a matter of course that the children of pious parentage shall be heirs of everlasting life. Our Lord Jesus gives us the express and serious warning that many from distant lands shall enter heaven, while many children of the kingdom shall be cast out. Many a washed Naaman shall be accepted, many a leprous Gehazi rejected. One of our Lord's own disciples was a Judas, while he commended the faith of Gentiles.

What, then, is the profit of hearing so plainly the teachings of God's word? Much every way. But this word is no talisman to be placed unread upon the parlour table or hung as a charm around a careless neck. Gehazi's guilt was the greater because he knew so much better what he should do, and sinned against light so clear. Had he listened to the instructions he received, his end had not been this. It was not the fault of Elisha nor of the opportunities Gehazi enjoyed. It was his own sin and folly. He chose his way; it was earthly and sinful, and it disappointed him. But the advantages he possessed were not in advance of those that are now given to many in our own land. Indeed a greater than Elisha teaches us, and we read the records of miracles of grace more wonderful and attractive than even Naaman's cure. But the same principle rules now as then. It is not the mere possession, it is the due and humble improvement of our privileges, that secures the soul's salvation. And let us not forget that the soul may be lost when yet we do not imitate the particular form of Gehazi's sin. We may not defraud another of his goods, nor fill our mouths with such falsehoods as his. But, great as our advantages are, we must not rest upon them. They must lead us to Christ; we must flee from every iniquity and take him as our Saviour; we must be washed from our sins in his precious blood, or no weight will be heavier upon our heads to sink us to destruction than the oppressive consciousness that our privileges have been neglected and abused. Our Lord's language is, that those who have been exalted to heaven shall be cast down to hell if they repent not when so plainly taught.

CHAPTER XII.

ANGELIC MINISTRIES.

IT is pleasing to find so many intimations that the great work of Elisha's life increases upon his hands. In the great decline of religion through the wickedness of the Israelitish kings, no more effectual method could be adopted to counteract the prevailing evils than to raise up a new set of teachers; and the schools of the prophets appear to have secured an increasing number of pupils. So we read now, respecting the school established at Gilgal, that their accommodations were found too narrow; and they represented their case to the prophet, and desired his approbation of measures that looked to the enlargement of the institution. The matter is too briefly recorded to give us a full understanding of it. Whether there was an entire removal of the college from Gilgal to the Jordan, the distance being perhaps six miles, or whether they sought timber on the river banks to be carried to their present site, we cannot decide. We see the poverty of his disciples in that they must make these changes with their own manual labour, and that even the tools with which they wrought were borrowed. Quite likely they were unskilful workmen, and want of skill or accident gave occasion for recording another of the prophet's wonders. An axe-head fell into the Jordan, doubtless in too deep a place to admit of its recovery. The lamentation of the young man who lost it over an article that did not belong to him led the prophet to recover it by causing the iron to swim. The manner of doing this agrees with the usual practice of Elisha—by some external sign. The chief object may have been to confirm the faith of a new company of disciples in the extraordinary qualifications of their chief teacher.

We now read of new wars between Israel and Syria, and of Elisha's aid afforded to the king of Israel. The name of the new general of the Syrian army is afterward given; Naaman seems to have lost his place after his return from Samaria. The various plans formed by the king of Syria were supernaturally known to Elisha, and he made them known to the Israelitish leaders. In war, great advantages must ever belong to a bold assailant, who learns as nearly as possible the position and numbers of his enemies, and by concentrating his forces strikes a sudden and unexpected blow. The assailant generally knows his own aim—the attacked are confused by the necessity of guarding against dangers that are magnified because they are not comprehended. If the plans and time of attack are known, it is usually an easy thing to act upon the defence. Elisha made known the plans of the enemy and saved the forces of Israel. This was done so often that the king of Syria believed there must be some traitor in his camp. But when a council of officers was called to deliberate upon this matter, one of them solved the perplexity by declaring that Elisha had revealed everything, and could tell their most secret thoughts. The name of Elisha was a familiar one in their ears since Naaman's cure, and no man was disposed to question this solution of the matter.

It seems strange, however, that in such a case the king should make any effort to lay hold upon the prophet. If Elisha knew every plan that was formed against his people, would he not also know every plan formed against himself? How could the king expect to succeed in this enterprise? Yet how constantly do men fight against a greater than Elisha—even Elisha's God—as if he could ever be ignorant of the plans they form, could ever lack skill to thwart their wisest devices, or could ever fail to effect all his holy purposes, no matter what is the array of human wickedness against him! But the prophet teaches the Church a lesson of divine protection from the king's folly. Benhadad sent messengers to learn where the prophet was, and found him in Dathan, about twelve miles from Samaria. He then sent a considerable force of men, who passed by night to the place, and by the morning surrounded it with their chariots and horsemen. It would have been a very easy thing for Elisha to have avoided the danger entirely, but he would give us a better lesson. The servant of the prophet was doubtless Gehazi's successor, and though he reverenced his master, he had not acquired the full confidence which results from longer experience. When he arose in the morning and saw the city encompassed by a hostile army, he was greatly distressed.

The prophet took two methods of relieving the young man's distress: *First,* he comforted him by the assurance that more powerful protection was afforded to them; and *next,* he prayed that the young man's eyes might be opened to see for himself the host of their protectors. So the Lord opened the eyes of the young man, and "behold, the mountain was full of chariots and horses round about Elisha."

Here we have two distinct things for our instruction: *First,* we may notice the actual safety of these servants of God; and *next,* the recognition of this safety by the younger at the prayer of Elisha. The young man and Elisha were just as safe before the chariots and horses of fire were revealed, as they were afterward; yet the young man no longer feared when he saw. Here we have something that remains permanently true for the servants of God, and something granted specially for the occasion.

It remains true for all ages that they that are

for God are not feeble and few compared with the number and power of their enemies. It seems so many times. The world seems often given over to iniquity. In great matters revolutions often occur, troublous times arise, things seem all to go wrong, and men's hearts fail them for fear of the changes that threaten against all their ideas of true advancement. In individual affairs we are thrown into great perplexity, we encounter unexpected distresses, we see no path of deliverance. So we cry with the servant of Elisha, Alas! how shall we do? But why may not the long experience of God's people teach us that these are lessons of faith? None of these perplexities can occur to us but under the divine ordering. He has often led his most faithful servants into straits, and delayed their deliverance until they are forced like Abraham to "hope against hope;" he has still shown his grace and wisdom and power in an opportune time. The enemies of Elisha seem to have gained an advantage when they succeeded in surrounding the city while he was still there; but the advantages gained by the enemies of religion are never any more real than theirs. It is quite impossible that any can ever fight against God, oppose his cause, or attack his servants, and prosper.

The great fact for our consolation in his service is to know that God governs the world. This he does completely without peradventure, without the slightest exception that can be possible or that can be imagined. There can therefore be no success against him or against anything he designs to protect. The believer may stand alone against a crowd of opposers, yet they that are for him outnumber them far. This, therefore, may ever be the believer's song—

"Fear not, though many should oppose,
For God is stronger than thy foes,
And makes thy cause his care."

Whatever we are called upon to believe as to the means adopted by infinite wisdom for carrying on his government, however much we may sometimes be perplexed to understand why any enemies to it are permitted to exist, are allowed to form plans so audacious, and are able to secure some seeming success which fills them with increasing boldness and causes the hearts of good men to fear, still the great consolation is in knowing that God reigns.

Yet it is to the divine glory that his rule includes and subordinates all inferior agencies; not destroying them, but using them. Let us not busy ourselves in wondering why God has not made the world otherwise than it is, nor in conjecturing that he might govern it differently; let us distinctly recognize that *as it is,* with its manifold agencies both of animate things and things inanimate, it is governed by its Creator; and that he is fully able, in his own good time, to vindicate all that he has allowed to occur and all that he has done in the orderings of his providence. Enough is constantly brought before us of the beneficence and kindness of his workings to show his mercy to man, while the wonderful leadings of his providence to bless men in unexpected measures give us profound ideas of God's wisdom. No matter what may be the instrument which he uses to further his designs, we are authorized to ascribe all to his working. Nor have we any reason to judge that any failures occur, any procrastination takes place, any mistakes are made in the completion of every design which divine wisdom has ever formed. When we look at the things we can best understand, we see the most unswerving exactness and punctuality observed. The sun never delays his time of rising or setting, and every variation in changing seasons occurs with the utmost regularity. The laws that govern inferior things around us are of such unchanging operation that any well-established instance of miracle is therefore also a well-established proof of divine working for a higher end than nature can reach. All things are the servants of their Creator. Fire and hail, rain and snow, and vapour, stormy wind fulfilling his word, all are his ministers. Even when men lose sight of the divine rule while they gaze upon the instrumentalities which God uses, it remains true that natural things, and all the laws by which they exist and operate, are subject to his government. His wisdom and power are everywhere. Without divine energy no existence could be or operate. In the language of the poet, this

> "Warms in the sun, refreshes in the breeze,
> Glows in the stars and blossoms in the trees;
> Lives through all life, extends through all extent,
> Spreads undivided, operates unspent."

There is one chapter concerning the government of the world which we read only in the sacred Scriptures. This chapter refers to the agency of angels in the world's providential rule. It is a deeply interesting thing to believe that

> "Millions of spiritual beings walk this earth,
> Unseen, both when we sleep and when we wake."

That the agency is invisible is not strange, since the most powerful agents in nature—gravitation, attraction, electricity—are known to man only by their unquestioned effects; and no man hath seen God at any time. It is not wonderful to believe that our Infinite God is the Creator of other intelligent beings besides the race of man. When we know that the stars are innumerable worlds like the earth on which we live, we think it reasonable to judge that he created them not in vain, but formed them to be inhabited, Isa. xlv. 18. And in the habitation of his own holiness we are assured that there are hosts of holy, intelligent beings, of powerful intellects and swift to do his will.

Especially are the angels of God employed in matters which pertain to the administration of the covenant of grace. They are therefore called ministering spirits, "sent forth to minister to them that shall be heirs of salvation." In all the great matters pertaining to the advancement of the Church of God, especially in the earlier dispensations, the angels bore a distinguished part. Perhaps, in the world before the flood, communication between heaven and earth was chiefly maintained by their ministry. And in a certain sense the Mosaic economy was a dispensation given by angels. That is, thousands of angels were present upon Sinai at the giving of the law, and angels rendered various important ministries during that age. It is also true in some sense that the Christian dispensation is not subject to the rule of angels, because the great Mediator has come in human nature. Heb. ii. Yet the angels are the obedient servants of Christ Jesus; they delight to do him homage, and the Church under his control is a Church where angels minister. If we read of them in the ancient times ascending and descending over Jacob's slumbers, delivering Lot from Sodom, and Jacob from Esau, and Daniel from the lions, slaying the first-born of Egypt in their houses and the hosts of the Assyrians in their camps, so we read of them in the New Testament times, rejoicing at the birth of the infant Saviour, ministering to him in his necessities and in his sorrows, and watching at his sepulchre. They attended at the ascension of the glorified Redeemer; they surround his throne now with ceaseless praises, save as they are sent to earth on errands of mercy; and when he comes a second time, in the glory of the judgment-throne, he will be accompanied by all the holy angels. What their duties are upon earth we may learn either from scriptural precepts or scriptural examples. They minister to the heirs of salvation; they encamp about them that fear God and deliver them; they rejoice over the return of the wandering prodigal. They enter the prison and give aid to the prisoner; they wait around the couch of those that are in distress and offer their unseen ministries; they are by the departing couch of the dying believer, though he may be like the beggar Lazarus in wretchedness, and they bear away the happy spirit to the bosom of Abraham. Christ is the Lord of angels. At his bidding they come and go. They are great in might and swift to do his will. When he sends they fly quickly; what he commands they do; the meanest saint they are ready to succour, the meanest service for him they are ready to perform. These hosts are *for* God's people, and they far outnumber all who can be *against* them.

"Here a bright squadron leaves the skies,
  And thick around Elisha stands;
Anon a heavenly soldier flies,
  And breaks the chain from Peter's hands.
Are they not all thy servants, Lord?
  At thy command they go and come;
With cheerful haste obey thy word,
  And guard thy children to their home."

WATTS.

If we do not often engage our thoughts respecting angels and their service toward the earthly Church, it is not because the Scriptures are too silent respecting them. "A multitude of writers in the Scriptures—*fifteen at least*—have described these glorious beings with the most perfect harmony and without a single discordant idea."* Christians should think with pleasure of angelic ministries.

> "How oft do they their silver bowers leave,
> To come to succour us that succour want! . . .
> They for us fight, they watch and duly ward,
> And their bright squadrons round about us plant,
> And all for love, and nothing for reward." †

They are now our guardians; they shall be our eternal associates. They have watched us thus far through all our pathway on earth; they know our history better than we know it ourselves; they are constantly about us; and they have doubtless given us protection and the victory many a time when we knew not of their care. Shall we believe that evil is suggested to the human mind by satanic temptations, and reject the thought that we may receive strength from the angels whom Christ sends to minister to his people? Angelic services are constantly rendered; their hosts encamp around us; they can tell us, when we meet on the heavenly plains, most interesting events of our own lives that were wholly secret to us while we were here below.

* Dwight's Theol., i. 313.

† See first two stanzas Spenser's Faery Queen, Bk. ii., Canto viii.

Some have been of the opinion that each person has a particular guardian angel assigned to him, who attends him through all the course of his life, to watch over, protect, guide and warn him; the Mohammedans extend the doctrine so that each has a good and a bad angel—the one protecting, the other devising evil. Two passages in the New Testament seem to refer to the doctrine of a good guardian angel, yet are they not sufficiently explicit to establish it. Our Lord says, "Take heed that ye offend not one of these little ones, for I say unto you that in heaven their angels do always behold the face of my Father which is in heaven," Matt. xviii. 10. This passage teaches that the youngest and meanest of the disciples of Christ is under the guardianship of angels, but does not confine their protection to a single guardian for each. When Peter was delivered from prison, and the disciples could not credit his appearance, they said, It is his angel! Their words contain an evident reference to the prevalent Jewish opinion, not only of a special guardian to each individual, but of one whose form resembles him whom they are set to guard. But the passage may but show that these disciples still retained the ideas they formerly held, without proving, in the absence of direct teachings, that this opinion is scriptural. In the case of Elisha we see that many angels were round about the prophet for his protection.

The angels of God are constantly about us. Paul

seems to teach especially that they are ever present in the worshipping assemblies of God's people; and we have reason to judge that men are perpetually in the sight of angels. The invisible, eternal world is not far off from us. In our perplexities and distresses we may be often ready to say, Alas! how shall we do? Yet our deliverers are not far off. True, we cannot discern them with our natural senses, for this is not their capacity. And we cannot even conjecture what intuitive knowledge of the most satisfactory nature might be gained if we possessed the proper faculties. A man born blind cannot possibly know, even though we should attempt to explain it, what light is, and what wondrous revelations light gives to the seeing eye. One glance of perfect vision would avail more to awaken and inform the soul than centuries of instruction upon the wonderful properties of light. So Elisha prays for his servant, Lord, I pray thee, open his eyes, that he may see. This is the view the Scriptures give us of the spiritual world, that it is as much about us as above us; that angels ascend and descend between earth and heaven on errands from their Lord; and that more and stronger are for the believer than can be arrayed against him. What though our eyes are not opened to see, as were the eyes of the prophet's servant? The divine rule is unchanged still, and will remain so for ever. The God who then protected his servant in peril by unseen hosts still allows his people to fall into seen dangers and protects them by unseen guardians.

This entire doctrine of unseen spiritual influences has also its fearful aspects. For there are unseen tempters to evil. Our warfare is with spiritual wickedness. Satan and his angels are ever about us. The invisible things around us, both good and evil, are of great influence upon us. Yet the evil can never force us to evil; they can but suggest and tempt, and they are restrained in various ways. They who put their trust in Christ Jesus, the Lord of angels, need never fear. For thus runs the promise to the believing: "He shall give his angels charge over thee to keep thee in all thy ways; they shall bear thee up in their hands, lest thou dash thy foot against a stone," Ps. xci. 11, 12. Was Elisha safe in Dothan when the chariots of God were around him? The Syrians saw them not. His servant did not see them till the prophet prayed that he might. But his safety depended upon their being present, not upon their being visible. And a thousand providences in the history of God's people show unexpected deliverances that have been effected by ministering angels. No matter that we cannot see. The God of angels pledges his people a full protection; and these are cheerful servants, swift to do his will.

But we return now to the narrative. Elisha further prayed that the Lord would smite the Syrians with blindness. We do not suppose that they were really made blind, so that they could not see at all. In that case, they would hardly have ventured to march to Samaria. For we can scarcely conceive of an army of blind men and blind horses being able to make a march at all. But as the opening of the eyes of Elisha's servant was not enabling him to see the invisible hosts with his bodily eyes—which perhaps is as impossible as to hear a colour or to see a sound—but rather giving him a knowledge of their presence, which for want of a fitting term we call *seeing* or *perceiving*, so the blindness of the Syrian hosts was rather giving false perceptions. They saw, but not as things really were: they neither recognized Dothan nor the prophet. The words of the prophet are evidently the answer to a question put by the Syrians. Taken by themselves, they seem to be falsehood upon the prophet's lips. We know indeed that many of the ancient believers were rather governed by the low standard of morals prevalent in their times than by the strict rule of unswerving truth to which alone the precepts of the Scriptures give their sanction. To use falsehood in the stratagems of war has been regarded as allowable in the teachings of all other moralists, even including many Christian writers. But no explicit sanction of any falsehood can be found in the word of God: on the contrary, the Scriptures approve of truth, and this so entirely beyond exception or apology that if we judge any man at any time guilty of falsehood, we must condemn it. Elisha was not without his infirmities, though indeed we would not expect him to speak untruly at such a time. And there seems no need of it. Falsehood is generally a confession of weakness. When men can reach the end they seek as easily, they speak the truth, having no object to deceive. Elisha had these men in his power without speaking any untruth. The whole matter depends upon what the question was to which Elisha's words were a reply. If they asked, Where shall we find Elisha? the prophet, though he stood before them, could truly answer, Not this way, and not this city; for he intended to let them see him only at Samaria. They were deceived indeed by these words, but the law of truth does not require a man to correct the false conceptions of his enemies.

Elisha led these hosts to Samaria. They were under the influence of these false perceptions until they were in the very city, and were surrounded by the hosts of the king of Israel in such numbers as to make resistance hopeless. Then their eyes were opened and they saw their position. The king of Israel, out of deference to the power of the prophet who had delivered these men into his hands, asked Elisha's advice respecting the disposal of the prisoners. At his direction no cruelty was exercised upon them: they were kindly treated as prisoners of war, and soon released to return to their own land. Peace was soon made between

Israel and Syria. It seemed in vain for the king of Syria to expect success against a people thus protected. And indeed the guilt of Israel alone exposed them to further wars. We soon read of new strifes and of new success on the part of Syria, for Jehoram and his people would not learn repentance, either from the Lord's judgments or mercies.

CHAPTER XIII.

THE SIEGE AND DELIVERANCE OF SAMARIA.

WE are not able to judge with any accuracy respecting the lapse of time between the various events recorded here. We would suppose that after a defeat so remarkable, succeeded by such an act of clemency, the king of Syria would allow at least some years to pass away before he renewed his warfare against Israel. But when two neighbouring nations have been at war with each other, and come to look upon each other almost as natural enemies, it takes but small offence to renew their conflicts. Of this most unhappy tendency of our sinful nature we have but too many examples. At this period Israel and Syria were rival kingdoms, easily embroiled with each other; and the barbarous style of their warfare exasperated both parties, so as to separate them more widely. Yet the records of cruelty all belong to the Syrians, who repay badly the generous conduct already mentioned on the part of Jehoram. (Compare 2 Kings vi. 22, 23 and viii. 12; x. 32.)

This time the war was carried to the gates of Samaria, and the attempt was made, as was common in ancient warfare, to reduce the city by starvation. The ancient engines of war were often utterly powerless against well-fortified places, and a siege was a tedious affair. Of course the length of time necessary to reduce a garrison by famine would depend upon the supplies that had been laid in in preparation for such a time. The king of Israel bravely maintained the defence of his capital city until reduced to great extremity. The instances given in the narrative to prove the scarcity of provisions have given great perplexity to commentators. "An ass's head was sold for fourscore pieces of silver, and a fourth part of a cab of doves' dung for five pieces of silver." So far as the general meaning of the passage is concerned, there is no difficulty in deciding that it is intended to denote the great scarcity of food in the city. Some suppose that "an ass's head" signifies the whole animal, as we say "so many head of cattle;" but the famine was greatly more distressing if we understand it literally. No scruples could be made at such a time as that because the flesh of the ass was not reckoned clean by the Israelites, since people who were driven to other extremities here mentioned would forget all the requirements of a ceremonial law. It is a very common opinion that the *doves' dung* here mentioned was a kind of grain or pulse which has some resemblance to the dung of the dove. This is dried as we dry beans and peas, and stored for use on long journeys. Yet it is said that if the language be taken literally, other similar records can be found in other histories.

We do not need to dwell upon the dreadful description afterward given in this narrative. It sets the horrors of the siege before us in a light far surpassing that shown by any prices paid for ordinary or unusual food. Yet the horrible atrocity of eating human flesh and of parents eating their own children has been too often repeated in the history of the race to make it surprising here. This is among the sufferings predicted by Moses which should come upon the sons of Jacob because of their sins against God, Deut. xxxiii. 53–57. Josephus records an example fulfilling this prediction during the memorable siege of Jerusalem by Titus and the Romans. He speaks of it as quite unparalleled in human history, and indeed it so remains until now, though he himself had elsewhere recorded the similar instance in this siege of Samaria, and other historians give similar accounts of other sieges. Doubtless the people of Samaria had never heard of such a case before; and if, when the tidings spread through their city that in their distress a mother had slain aud eaten her own child, they recalled the solemn warning of their lawgiver, they must have entertained a deep impression of their guilt as drawing upon them the woes he had denounced.

We cannot but respect some characteristics of the king of Israel at this time. He was an idolater, and kept too close to the ways of Ahab his father, being perhaps greatly under the influence of Jezebel, who was still living. But he was a brave warrior, and his endurance of this siege for so long a time marks his firmness and his power over a people nearly grown desperate. At this time it may be he had some relentings for his evil courses, and knew that these judgments upon him were from the true God of his people. He heard the complaint of one of his people as he passed around the walls, doubtless making personal observations of the strictness with which a watch was maintained, and declared that unless Jehovah helped all help was in vain. At the horrible tale told in his ears the king rent his clothes, and the bystanders, to their great surprise, noticed that he had sackcloth under his royal robes and next his flesh. Here is some evidence of sincerity in the king's penitence. Doubtless it was not that profound and genuine grief that forsakes sin, as well as bows under the rod for it; true repentance is always permanent, and we have too good proof that Jehoram loved not the service of Jehovah. Yet he was truly grieved, and this not for a show before his people. He rent his clothes from a sudden impulse of tidings so fearful suddenly given, but the sackcloth under his robes was accidentally revealed.

It is not an easy thing for us to decide how sincere and how deep may be that species of penitence which yet is not godly sorrow. Men may weep for their sins, they may make profuse promises of reformation, they may sincerely purpose that they will do iniquity no more, yet may their goodness be "as the morning cloud and as the early dew," Hos. vi. 4. True repentance differs from false in something else besides the mere sincerity of our regrets. It refers to the nature of our regrets—that they spring not from the mere trouble our sins have brought upon us, but from the shamefulness of our guilt. The dishonest man may not steal for fear of discovery and punishment; the honest man will not, because of the wrong involved. Sorrow for our sins is not genuine unless we have a true sense of sin as in itself shameful and evil, and unless our turning from it is a true turning to its opposite in the service of the Lord. The king of Israel may have been sincere in this sense, that while he humbled himself by wearing sackcloth, he made no hypocritical show of this to attract the public attention; what he did was before God and was accidentally discovered to man; yet his was a sincerity of grief, rather than of penitence. We do not wonder to find inconsistencies mingling with his feelings and conduct. His anger is kindled against the prophet Elisha, and he swore that he would take the prophet's head. This was very unreasonable. The prophet was not responsible for any of these things. We may learn here and elsewhere in the Scriptures that the most remarkable prophets were servants, not able to work miraculous deliverances at their own will, but subject to divine direction and the impulses of the Holy Spirit. The same Elisha who multiplied the widow's oil, fed a hundred men with a few loaves and delivered the Assyrian host into the hands of Jehoram, now sits in his house and quietly suffers his share of the dread famine in Samaria. Elisha is no more than another man, except when the Spirit of God is upon him.

It was not Elisha's fault that famine ruled in Samaria. The true fault was in the evils of the house of Ahab, and the true remedy was a genuine penitence on their part. And it is very likely that Elisha had encouraged the king to maintain the siege, and had promised that God would send deliverance. It may have been through the prophet's exhortations that the king wore this sackcloth; and we know from the case of Ahab that God withholds his judgments when civil rulers honour him before their people, even though theirs is not a thorough penitence. (See 1 Kings xxi. 29.) It is not, however, strange that the king so severely threatens Elisha, and then as suddenly withdraws his threat. We know that in times of severe calamity the minds of men are often filled with a blind and sudden rage, and change fitfully from one thing to another. What feelings of anguish, revenge, fearfulness, rush through the minds of men in hurried succession upon tidings of a great calamity upon the battle-field. We are in a turmoil of passion. We may perhaps forecast these evils, yet we nerve ourselves in agitated, bitter, blind rage against we know not whom. So may it now have been with the king of Israel. Around him he saw the miserable proof that his capital was already at the last extremity, the wretched sentinels tottered on the walls they were set to watch, he himself, it may be, passed around on foot, for his chariot horses were unfit for service (viii. 13), and these last dreadful tidings of the severity of the distress filled the cup of his misery. If Elisha had promised deliverance, we can scarcely think strange that the wretched king should now feel that he could wait no longer. The delays of divine providence often try the patience of the best of men, and ungodly men like Jehoram often cut the knot by saying, We will wait no longer.

Yet God dealt with him and his people in great forbearance, and gave them his mercy in the extremity of their distress. Elisha sat in his house, surrounded by the elders; perhaps not the civil rulers of the city, but his disciples or the religious teachers of the people. He knew the message of the king, and gave orders that the messenger should be detained, for he would soon be followed by the king himself. He calls him the son of a murderer, for Ahab had slain the Lord's prophets and had caused Naboth to be put to death (1 Kings xviii., xxi.); and Jehoram in character followed too closely in his father's ways. Josephus says that the king relented of his first order, and came after his messenger to countermand it. The king's mind was evidently greatly agitated. He knew that these evils were a judgment of God upon him and his people; he is almost disposed to take all the revenge he can by depriving Elisha of life; but this, he knows, will be of no avail to deliver the city. Just in this extremity the prophet takes new occasion to predict deliverance, and even to set a definite and early time for it. He declared that within twenty-four hours the greatest plenty should reign there. The declaration seemed so utterly unlikely that it was received with incredulity, which, on the part of a chief officer of the king, found expression in words, and these words proved fatal to himself. He said, scoffingly, that unless the Lord would make windows in heaven this thing could not be; and the prophet answered him that he should see this thing, but have no share in it.

That same night deliverance came by unexpected means. The Syrian army was seized with a panic and fled. They heard, or imagined they heard, a great noise, as if a vast army was coming against them. We need not conjecture what really caused their alarm. For many ages the name *panic* has been given to that mysterious dread which sometimes fills large bodies of men from slight, indefinable causes, and which leads the boldest to seek instant and dastardly flight. Mythology says that the frightful god Pan, accompanying the army of Bacchus, relieved it from great danger by a wild scream, which, being repeated by the echoes of the woods and rocks, scared the enemy away. It was the belief of the ancients that to punish the presumption of men the gods often struck their armies during the night with a sudden terror. And instances of panics, that seem hard to account for, in the conduct of disciplined and brave troops, can easily be gathered by one well read in the history of either ancient and modern warfare.

It may be interesting to mention a few examples of these in modern times. In 1640, when the Scottish army attacked the forces of Charles I. at Newbern ford, the English were surprised by a sudden discharge of artillery; the whole army was seized with a panic; Sir Thomas Fairfax owned that his legs trembled under him until he passed the Tee; the forces at New Castle fled to Durham, and, not thinking themselves safe there, retreated precipitately to Yorkshire. So in the battle of Preston Pans in 1745, the English dragoons were so frightened by the fierce shouts of the Scottish Highlanders that they fled precipitately, headed by their commander, who was afterward congratulated as being the first general that ever carried the tidings of his own defeat. This was in the war made by the Pretender for the recovery of the English crown; and Dr. Witherspoon, in a speech made in the Continental Congress, declares that the English militia then behaved fifty times worse than any American militia in the Revolutionary war, for they generally disbanded and ran off wholly as soon as the enemy came within ten or twenty miles of them. In 1810, during the Peninsular war, when Massena, flushed with victory, was advancing upon Lisbon, a singular incident of this kind occurred among a choice body of British troops. They were under the command of General Crawford, had been the dread of the French and the pride of the British, and only a year before had signalized their discipline and courage in a masterly retreat of sixty miles from the field of Talavera. But on the 23d of September, 1810, they were sleeping on their arms in a wood, when from some unknown cause the entire division fled from their bivouac like a flock of sheep; and neither threats nor remonstrances from their officers could induce them to form into ranks, until a young officer sounded a cavalry charge in their front. Then the men mechanically formed into squares, to be ready to receive the imaginary foe.

In still later days, during the Italian war, a panic occurred in a whole reserve *corps d'armée* of the French forces, and the account is given us by the Hon. Mr. R——, the editor of a prominent American journal, who was there, partook of the fright and ran himself with the fugitives. Five Austrians, whose retreat was cut off, rode rapidly into the village where the reserve forces were stationed, with the design of giving themselves up. The frightened inhabitants cried out, "The Austrians are coming!" and ran for their lives. The soldiers followed suit; horse, foot and dragoons, pell mell, without waiting to take care of the wounded, ran fifteen miles without stopping. One wounded French general offered a large reward to be carried to a place of safety. Mr. R—— confesses to have run ten miles on foot before he stopped.

A panic among the loyal troops in the first battle of Bnll's Run in the recent American civil conflict, if not the cause of their defeat, greatly aggravated the disasters of the battle.

The whole army of the Syrians fled for their lives. So terror-stricken were they that they did not even attempt to use the very agencies of a more speedy flight, but they even left their horses and asses tied in their places, while the men rushed away as if frantic. And, just as soldiers usually do at such a time, as they ran they gradually disencumbered themselves, flinging away clothes, arms, vessels, everything that burdened them and hindered their hasty flight.

The discovery of this to the Israelites was made in the night, and through no watchfulness of Jehoram's sentinels. Four leprous men sat in the gate of Samaria considering their own helpless condition. Perhaps at such a time as that the rigid exclusion of these unfortunate persons from the city could not be insisted upon, for that would result in driving them forth into the hands of the enemy —a cruelty which the law of Moses cannot be thought to have contemplated. But if they had access to the city—as their words may perhaps imply—they would be permitted to come there only through pity—a pity that in the present state of Samaria would extend only to protection and not to supply of their wants. These unhappy men pondered their miserable condition, and saw that they might pursue one of three plans, all of which seemed desperate, yet not equally so: *First*, they might sit still where they were, but they had nothing to eat, and they must certainly die. *Secondly*, they might try to enter the city. If permitted to do this, they must still starve, for they had no money, and provisions would be given only to those who were available for fighting, and certainly not to lepers. *Thirdly*, they might go forth to the enemy and throw themselves upon their protection. But it was most unlikely that the Syrians would spare the lives of lepers, or, after sparing, also feed them. Yet this was the only direction in which they could see a ray of light; the most that could be said was, that all other resources were desperate, and this was not quite so. At the worst they could but die, and they would venture this.

So these poor men, who seem to have been outside of the line of sentinels, or who were at least allowed to pass unchallenged, took their way to the hostile camp. There, too, they found none to stay them. The camp was deserted. It was in the dusk of the evening that they reached there, and the Syrians had perhaps just gone. Confusion and disorder were everywhere, and doubtless the first act of the lepers was to satisfy their hunger. Then they seized upon spoil enough to make them rich, and hid it lest it should be wrested from them. The Jews say that these lepers were Gehazi and his three sons; and surely here is enough to satisfy the most covetous capacity. But there were also better sentiments in the minds of these men. Actuated by good impulses perhaps, and perhaps by some superstitious feeling that if they kept all this to themselves they might incur some special frown of Providence—rather a salutary species of superstition—the lepers bethought themselves and resolved to tell the people of Samaria of the flight of the enemy. This was a day of good tidings, and others should share their joy. They had perhaps spent several hours of the night in eagerly securing the advantages so unexpectedly set before them; but this better feeling sent them back to Samaria.

There they called to the keepers of the gates and gave them tidings none the less welcome because told by leprous lips. The news was good enough to be told in the ears of the king, and he was roused from his slumbers for that purpose. It is little to the credit of King Jehoram that he was not prepared to believe this, even though Elisha had so recently proclaimed a speedy and complete deliverance. We could not expect the king to imagine that the help would come thus, but he ought to have been prepared for good tidings in some form. But Jehoram will not credit the report of the lepers. Yet one of his advisers suggested that in their desperate circumstances it would at least be well to send out explorers who could go far enough to learn the truth. If, as the king feared, the Syrians were but playing with their necessities, this could soon be ascertained. A few horses were still left to them that were able to go upon such an expedition. They took the advice of this counsellor, and they found the rout as complete as they could desire. The whole distance to the Jordan bore marks of the hasty flight of the enemy; nothing was destroyed before their departure; the entire spoil of their enemies fell into the hands of the garrison of Samaria.

The glad news soon spread through the famished city, and the delivered people went out to refresh themselves with the food they so much needed. The king took possession of the whole, and appointed the same officer who had disbelieved the prophet's words upon the previous day to have charge of the distribution. And this appointment was the means of fulfilling the reply of the prophet to him, that he should not partake of the plenty. Either that he was imperious beyond what the people could brook in a time of so great a necessity, or that the accidental pressure of the hungry multitude crushed him as he sat in the gate to execute his commission, so it was that they trod upon him and he died. The prophet's words were fulfilled. Less than twenty-four hours had passed from the period of greatest scarcity, and now bread was sold plentiful and cheap in the gate of the city.

The interesting narrative recorded in the seventh chapter may suggest many profitable thoughts. Among them we may briefly dwell upon a few.

The judgment of these leprous men that they did wickedly in keeping to themselves the good tidings that were so needed in the distressed city, expresses the just feeling which should dwell in every ingenuous mind. If the providence of God has freely given us his bounties, and there are others within our reach who stand in pressing need, our very abundance in contrast with their poverty is a call upon us to impart to them if we would have the divine blessing upon what we enjoy. It is not in the selfish use of anything that we can find its best advantages. Freely ye have received, freely give. If God has given us the gospel and its precious teachings, it is not for our exclusive use. We, poor lepers, have been mercifully led to find food and healing, and can we keep to ourselves the good things of God's grace when the necessities of a race lying in the darkness and misery of paganism are known to us—when these precious teachings can disperse their gloom and fill them with everlasting joy, and when indeed we have received these great blessings accompanied by the command to send them forth to others in all the earth? With us it is a day of good tidings—with them are ignorance and despair. If we withhold good from them to whom it is due when it is in the power of our hand to do it, will not He that keeps our soul know it? If we sit still until the morning, will not mischief follow our selfish breach of duty? We may take our lessons from the past experience of God's people. The Church at large, or any individual believer or body of believers, will prosper in their own precious experience just in proportion as they make earnest, careful efforts to impart also to others the great blessings they enjoy. No intelligent Christian can doubt that the modern missionary efforts of the Church have proved a great blessing to the Church; and no professors of religion give better proof of piety, enjoy more the comforts and evidences of religion, or do more to win the respect of even opposers, than those who are most zealously engaged in spreading abroad the teachings of the gospel. Like the traveller likely to perish from cold who saved his own life by his exertions to save a freezing companion, a double good is done by every Christian effort: we get good by doing good, and the price of indolent and selfish inactivity is the shrivelling of our own power and the failure of our comforts.

See how it is in times of awakened interest in

the Church! How sinful for men not to tell others of the Lord's grace! and how does the Church flourish when with thankful hearts we desire to tell to the perishing the great things of his mercy! The blessing of God upon us is the divine direction to seek to bless others, and they may anticipate mischief who refuse obedience.

But we may illustrate from the reasoning of these leprous men the estate and the duty of sinful souls who ponder the question. Why sit we here until we die? Not, as with these men, the life of the body is in jeopardy, but the life of the soul. Why sit ye here all the day idle? may the Lord of the vineyard say to many who hear the teachings of the gospel. Suppose we consider the condition of a sinful soul as it often seems to the awakened and anxious mind. It is much like the case of these lepers at Samaria's gate. Let the three things they pondered be noticed also here. The gate of the city may be the sinner's present estate. If he sits still he must die. If it is possible for him even to remain as he is, he is unreconciled to God and must perish. The city may represent the guilty world into whose follies and sins he may plunge yet more deeply than ever before. But this is also the road to death. No hope is in either of these things. If he could sit still, he should not. Go farther away from God he should not; in these things are despair and death. Yet it seems to him that God will not hear. He is angry with him; his just wrath forbids such a sinner to approach and seek salvation. But even in this worst view of the case, here is the only ray of hope. As these leprous men saw no ray of light save in the bare possibility that the Syrians would pity and spare, so the sinner may be certain of perishing if he does not fly to Christ. Why should he not then act upon this serious reflection? "It may be that the Lord will pity." When Jonah preached the destruction of Nineveh, the king called the people to repentance, saying, "Who can tell if God will repent and turn away from his fierce anger, that we perish not?" Jon. iii. 9. In the very worst aspect of his case why should not the sinful soul say,

"I can but perish if I go,
I am resolved to try;
For if I stay away, I know
I must for ever die?"

What is to be gained by giving up to despair while life is still given, and the faintest hope remains that we can secure so great a thing as the soul's eternal life?

But though sinful men often feel that their condition is nearly desperate, we are not willing to admit that the gospel so represents the case. If these leprous men had received a message from the Syrians, bidding them come to the camp and they should find plenty, or if two of their number had gone and been kindly received, and then had returned to tell the other two, we can easily judge that new hopes would urge these others to go hastily forth. Now sinful men are invited to come to Christ for life. True, they often perversely argue that the calls of the gospel do not mean them, and that the promises of the gospel they dare not appropriate. But they ought to know that many a fellow-sinner, who has felt and argued just as they do now, has timidly ventured to draw near the mercy-seat, and that this trembling faith has not been sent empty away. Encouragements may be found to lead the most guilty and the most dejected to look to Christ. And surely they are wretched and foolish who consider the various possible things they may attempt and choose the very worst they can. Sinful souls must repent or perish. They cannot increase their sins without aggravating their doom; they cannot neglect the gospel and not stand in greater danger. What though they do have their fears that such as they may be rejected? Yet they must find Christ or perish. And *he* says he will in no wise cast out. Having never rejected any, will he begin with you? Found of so many that have not sought him, will he not be found also of them "that diligently seek him?"

CHAPTER XIV.

ELISHA'S INTERVIEW WITH HAZAEL.

THE hasty glances we are able to give in this brief history at the changing thoughts of the king of Syria may remind us of the impressions that religion makes upon ungodly men in every age. At one time the king wars against Israel; at another, applies there for help to relieve a valuable servant; at one time sends to take Elisha a prisoner, at another, makes humble supplication to the honoured prophet. If sinful men in the world around us would but follow out their own best impulses, keep the promises they make in serious and thoughtful hours, and maintain consistently the character they sometimes assume, it would be to their own infinite advantage and to the welfare of all around them. But the serious thoughts and the anxious applications of the king of Syria had really little influence upon his general character: in trouble he asked for help where he thought he could secure it, but he had no more true drawings to Elisha's principles at one time than another. And men may live all their lives in a Christian land, respectful to religious principles and religious teachers, convinced that they need the blessings which religion alone can bestow, and sometimes half persuaded to seek for the offered mercies of the gospel, and yet they may pass through the world and die at last as truly separated from the people of God as the king of Syria was separated from the kingdom of Israel with which he was so often at war. The inconsistencies of men often serve the purpose of deluding them with flattering hopes, yet they ought to teach them most profitable lessons. Men who make occasional promises to religion have certainly no good excuse for its neglect, since thus they prove their persuasion of religious excellency, and declare their own folly in pursuing paths not approved by their own consciences.

Benhadad's lessons hitherto have been lost upon him. Naaman, it may be, is banished from the court, for gratitude to Israel stands in no high repute at Damascus. Yet we shall soon see that the king made a poor exchange when Hazael became the leader of Syria's armies. After the panic at the siege of Samaria it is likely that peace was made between the kingdoms: seven years have passed since that—years of famine upon the land, double as long as in the days of Elijah; and of these we have no record, except the incident already noticed (chap. viii.) of the restoration of the lands of the Shunamite. At this time Elisha came to Damascus, perhaps to fulfil the command long since given to Elijah and to declare, if not to anoint, Hazael king of Syria. (See 1 Kings xix. 15.) Just then Benhadad fell sick. Kings and nobles of the earth are as other men. As vainly as Canute ordered back the advancing tide of the ocean, as vainly as the Persian monarchs would forbid the entrance of sorrow to their palaces, would the kings of the earth attempt to ward off grief from their sacred persons; and when sorrow comes they are as weak as other men. Afflictions often teach men lessons they are otherwise unwilling to learn, bring thoughts and convictions they are usually wont to suppress, and lead them to honour principles they have affected to despise. Benhadad heard that Israel's illustrious prophet had come to Damascus. He remembered now the great cure wrought for Naaman, and he determined to send and ask what should be the issue of his own sickness. We may see here that he did not ask a cure: he had not the faith for that. But believing that Elisha could penetrate the secrets of futurity, he inquires the prospects of his recovery.

He sent Hazael, doubtless his chief minister, in great state to ask the prophet. As was customary in coming before the prophets—as indeed is the usual Oriental courtesy—he brought with him large presents, but we are not informed this time whether Elisha did or did not accept them. The prophet gave a singular but most truthful reply. The oracular responses of pagan priests were famous for ambiguity. "I tell you, O son of Eacus, that you the Romans can conquer," was the answer given to Pyrrhus, so cunningly constructed that the grammar will justify either interpretation of the things that must occur—the Romans can conquer you, or you can conquer the Romans. Elisha's reply was ambiguous only as a riddle is—the solution suits it as nothing else can. "Thou mayest certainly recover;" that is, the disease itself was not mortal. "Howbeit the Lord hath showed me that he shall surely die;" that is, by other means his death should certainly occur. There is no more obscurity in the reply than necessarily belongs to any event predicted as certain in itself, but left unexplained as to the means by which it shall be accomplished. And even as to this, Elisha immediately adds the proof that the manner of Benhadad's death was no secret to him.

He looked steadfastly into the face of the king's messenger until Hazael blushed and Elisha wept. The most reasonable solution of this scene lies in the conscious guilt of the Syrian and the upright boldness of the prophet. Yet Elisha's reproving look is dictated by a heart that compassionates guilt as well as rebukes it. What a contrast there is between these two men! See the mockery of Hazael, both toward his master and toward Elisha—toward man and toward God! He came with all the state and ceremony of Syrian grandeur to ask whether Benhadad would recover, while his own plot was already formed to sit upon a throne which he had resolved should so soon be vacant. He came before Israel's prophet, perhaps secretly deriding the answer he awaited with such a show of gravity, for he believed not that Elisha knew his secret thoughts or could see as far into the future as, upon this one point, Hazael's ambitious plans enabled him to see. Possibly he was startled when the prophet's words proved him a deceiver, and then his bold wickedness was no match for the eye of the holy man who knew his coming guilt. The prophet looked him out of countenance. There was a meaning in the look which guilt could not face. But the weeping of Elisha astonished him. He might have gone away, abashed and humbled at the voice of reproof, but the tears of his venerable reprover are beyond his understanding. He asked in surprise the meaning of this. He may have thought the death of the Syrian king no great subject for sorrow in an Israelitish prophet, and in Elisha's reply this is not put first forward. He spoke of the troubles Hazael should bring upon his people, of the atrocity of his wars, of his cruelty to the defenceless. These were things which as yet Hazael has not contemplated, nor can he believe they will ever be done by his orders. Then Elisha told him that he should be king over Syria. This soon took place. When Hazael returned, Benhadad asked him what message had been sent by Elisha. He answered in a direct falsehood, declaring that the prophet had foretold his certain recovery.

Perhaps Hazael would have given such a reply, even if he had formed no design against the king's life. Truth is seldom spoken in palaces, and it is the folly and the fault of monarchs that this is so. Indeed it is the fault of our common humanity, that we, none of us, like to hear unpleasant truths; so there is a temptation in the minds of those who would please us to hide unwelcome or painful truth from us. Kings often punish the bearers of unwelcome tidings, as if they brought the calamities they simply announce; and men who are not kings are unwilling to hear things they wish not to be true. So it happens that on a sick bed men are deceived until they die by the flatteries which their friends may or may not believe, but they dare not intimate to the sufferer any unpleasant anticipations. In the time of the king's sickness, unwelcome words touching his recovery would be carefully withheld from his ears. But it is likely that Hazael's plans were already formed for the monarch's death, and the false assurance of recovery, as if Elisha had said so, is designed to throw him off his guard. On the next day the king died. Taking advantage of his free access to his bed-chamber, either when they were alone, or when those were by whose interference he did not fear, he suffocated the sick man as he lay in his helplessness. Perhaps he was so prostrate that the process was easy; the people, aware of the king's feebleness, were not surprised to hear of his death;

no suspicion may have been awakened and no investigation made; and the reign of Hazael may have been undisturbed by any knowledge, on the part of his subjects, of his secret crime to reach the throne, as it is here recorded by the sacred writers. Thus on earth many a crime is unknown and passes without punishment; many a crime even elevates the offender; yet is a record made in a volume divinely written, to be openly published in due time.

But there are two interesting matters which should engage our attention as we read this narrative of the prophet's interview with Hazael. The first respects the possible influence of Elisha's words upon Hazael's crime; and the second, the evident unpreparedness now of Hazael for deeds of wickedness with which he afterward became familiar.

We are not expressly told that Hazael, when he came upon this errand of Elisha, had already formed his plot against the king's life. We infer this rather from the conduct of the prophet and the blush of conscious guilt that shrunk from Elisha's steadfast gaze. There are some who judge differently. These suppose that Elisha's prediction was the cause of its own fulfilment; that Hazael would perhaps not have thought of so great a crime as this but for this suggestion of it, accompanied by the assurance that it would prove successful; and that thus the prophet's words were even provocative of this man's subsequent career. We do not agree with this representation. But suppose it was so, suppose that Hazael never had thought of this crime until now—Elisha does not suggest it. He told him that he should be king over Syria. But if even he had told him that twenty years ago, in the desert of Sinai, God had bidden Elijah "anoint Hazael to be king over Syria" 1 Kings xix. 15, there would be in this no sanction for Hazael's iniquity as a means of reaching this predicted end. It is not the usual plan of God's dealings with the sons of men to inform them in advance of the events that are to occur in their lifetime. All these events are indeed spread open to his eye. "Known unto God are all his works from the beginning of the world" Acts xv. 18. It is in the infinite perfection of Jehovah that nothing can remain unknown to him in the illimitable future—that for everything there is an exact and appointed place in the unchangeable counsels of his wisdom. The settled plans of divine wisdom often give perplexity to shortsighted man. Men think that the very existence of divine counsels is wholly inconsistent with the freedom and responsibility of the creature, thus governed by the unchanging purposes of the Almighty. Yet this is to limit God, so that he can do only what man may understand. It is far more reasonable to judge that the freest liberty is secured to the intelligent creature *because* he is under the government of One who need stoop to no weakness that he may maintain his rightful authority.

The truth is, that God knows how to govern his

intelligent subjects so as to allow them the fullest exercise of their rational powers; that he is himself bound by the infinite and holy consistency of his own perfections to form only such plans as are wise, holy and just; and that there can be no wrong in carrying out such purposes as he would form into perfect and constant execution. There should be no more difficulty in conceding infinite excellency to all the divine plans than in granting that God's words are always true and God's workings are always right. His words and works are but the carrying out of his plans; all are agreeable to his holy nature; as to our Jehovah, "His work is perfect; for all his ways are judgment; a God of truth and without iniquity, just and right, is he." Deut. xxxii. 4. The counsels of God are no guide to the duty of man, since they are usually unknown to man. What we ought to do is made known in a different way.

If even God should make known to any man the future certainty of any particular event of his life, such knowledge should have no effect whatever in leading him to any departure from the plain path of holy obedience to God's righteous law. Rather such a man ought to argue that if such an event is sure to occur, it shall not be through any such means as shall lay upon him the responsibility of putting forth his hands to wickedness. When Elisha told Hazael that he should be king over Syria, and even intimated to him that the monarch, now so sick, would shortly die, why did not Hazael rather argue, "It is not worth my while to stoop to guilt, since I am sure, from the prophet's word, that I shall be king?" If this man put no trust in Elisha's word, then had it no influence upon his crime; if he did trust it, its legitimate influence was to lead him to rest secure of the issue, not perhaps with no care for the result, nor without any action at any time, but surely without any such words or conduct as would fill his new-gained honours with torturing remorse. In truth, such a declaration to Hazael was like the apparent openings of Providence around us all our lives; which are often but trials of our spirit, which are so clear intimations of the pathway of our duty, but which are themselves to be judged by the clearer teachings of God's word and God's law, that reveal to men his obligations. Neither does God's word nor his providence ever justify him who takes occasion from them to put forth his hand to sin.

We may find a very interesting, perhaps profitable, illustration of this whole matter if we compare the hasty crime of Hazael with the long forbearance of David under circumstances somewhat similar. David was living as a humble shepherd in his father's family when the prophet Samuel came at the Lord's bidding to the household of Jesse. The venerable man of God knew not himself upon which of the sons he should pour the anointing oil, but at the divine command he chose this one, the youngest of the whole; and from that time forward David knew that the crown and the throne of Israel must be his. But who can designate a single iniquitous or even impatient step taken by this anointed one to anticipate the counsels of God upon which he so fully relied? We would not know from the words or deeds of David that he had the most secret expectation of being the successor of Saul; he continued to be a loyal subject long after he felt oppressions that might make even "a wise man mad;" and when the world would have justified David in the destruction of his persecutor, he would not put forth his hand against the Lord's anointed. Every step from the sheepfold to the throne is taken by divine leadings, and not at the promptings of his own ambition. The reign of Saul was so violent, and especially so unjust for a long time to David himself, that there were many strong inducements to seek his death; if he had slain him upon several occasions, it would but be dealing with him upon the terms he himself had chosen; and it is very likely that David's reign might have been by several years longer, and no great reproach might have been cast upon him, if he had taken the life of a king of whose rule the people were tired and whom God himself had rejected. But David found no cause of sorrow, when the throne was reached at last, that he had no evil agency in Saul's casting down. His heart was as guiltless of treason against the kingdom as his hand was of the blood of the king; and it was David's joy as well as his honour that he waited the movements of divine providence. And had Hazael been truly faithful to his sick king, the words of Elisha could have been no suggestion of violence against his life. There is a sense in which men make themselves the course which then they attribute to the providence of God; the truth embracing all these things, that no man can plead any opportunities or even apparent beckonings of Providence as proofs that God approves a certain course, if yet undeniably he is passing on to violate the plain precepts of the divine law; that man's freedom is not only compatible with God's designs, but indeed secured by them; and that a just understanding of the government of God should lead us to expect the divine smile only upon blessings lawfully secured. And the subsequent career of Hazael, passing on to deeds of increasing cruelty, is proof that though Providence assigned him the crown of Syria, it was in no approval of either the man or his doings. The only proper method of interpreting the providences of God is to lay this truth at the foundation of all—that God's ways are consistent and harmonious. If the plainest possible opportunity arises for any man to speak falsely, to do wickedly or to secure any unjust advantage, he acts presumptuously who judges that Providence favours by affording the occasion. Providence tries the sons of men whether they will or will not keep the divine word, but if an angel from heaven should bid us do iniquity, we should refuse his bidding. There is no apology for Hazael, there is no complicity in Elisha, if even the announcement of his reign over Syria resulted in the death of Benhadad. And every man who attempts, in any measure, to lay his sin at the door of divine designs or divine providences is presumptuous as well as wicked. When men have tempting opportunities for gainful trade which yet are of evil tendency or imply evil doing, they may be sure that they are beckoned forward by PROFIT, not by PROVIDENCE.

But we designed to notice a second matter in the scene before us. Hazael evidently seems unprepared now for the career of wickedness to which he afterward went on. When the venerable prophet named the atrocities he should commit upon the people of Israel, Hazael was shocked; he could not think himself such a dog as to do things like these. And yet he did them. And we might allow the incident to pass with but a few words of wonder at the self-ignorance the Syrian betrays, if Hazael stood alone in such a case as this. But indeed he affords but one example, followed by thousands in every age since—not less in our own land than elsewhere—who have gone gradually on to form characters and to do deeds which in the earlier periods of life they themselves abhorred. It is wisdom for us to know that the ways of sin are ever deceitfulness, and that it is not as a matter of course, but as the result of careful and intelligent watchfulness and pains, that men keep themselves from the seductions of evil.

We do not know enough of the history of Hazael to enable us to trace the steps by which he passed onward. Yet these paths are so often trodden that we are at no loss to imagine why he should now be startled at the prophet's revelations, though he was hereafter to see their fulfilment. It is never by any deliberate purposes in advance that men become high-handed sinners. Indeed by no more remarkable thing is piety distinguished from impiety than by this—that seriously considering and patiently doing all a man should be and do will foster the principles and life of religion, while the most renowned among the wicked may reach their bad eminence through no deliberate designs. It may be that Hazael had but little idea of the task he undertook when he was ambitious of the throne, as indeed it may justly be affirmed that no man is able to "count the cost" when he embarks upon any career of evil. He who speaks one falsehood is often placed beyond his calculation in circumstances so embarrassing that another seems needful to hide the first, and these may grow to evils far greater than he designed. If Hazael had ascended the throne of Syria by right, he might have held his subjects by such bonds of allegiance and authority as would allow him to choose his own policy. But the wrong of the commencement placed him in a false position, and forced him perhaps to new crimes to maintain his power. If he had accomplices, they must be kept quiet; possibly his safety lay in giving the people something to do in a new war with Israel; it may be that the license given to his armies in the atrocities the prophet had predicted were the result of relaxed discipline in forces the usurper dare not too strictly control; or the gradual increase of evil may have made Hazael himself willing to do the most of these things. He who thought with horror of deeds that made Elisha weep in the very anticipation, became the terror of Israel, and remains to us an example to warn us against the increasing power of sin.

It is not an easy thing for us to explain—though it is a very easy thing for us to notice—that men by sin seem so to blunt their moral perceptions that they grow worse and worse, while yet they themselves become less concerned in growing evil. We know that men pass on from one degree of evil to another until they are utterly hardened in vice. Many a man whose first oath was uttered with a faltering tongue and a blushing cheek, speaks forth now the dreadful language of profanity with a bold brow. Many a man who first tasted the intoxicating glass with many misgivings of danger and degradation, has realized far more than he ever dreamed of, and yet now glories miserably in his own shame. The truth is, we are totally unable to comprehend the great things and the mean things, the good and the bad, to which the mind of man can be trained. How wonderful the skill that can be acquired in the various arts! how the hand and the eye and the mind can be schooled to things so beyond explanation that, if they were more uncommon, we would call them magical! How the printer can arrange the type, how the musician with inconceivable rapidity can touch accurately the most delicate note, how the jeweller discerns the precious stone, how every man in his own favourite sphere sees things that other eyes overlook, and does things that no one else knows how to do, and how do all these things become more easy as the habit is formed of doing them! Men cannot themselves explain whence arises their own judgment and skill and tact; things are done intuitively and are capable of no intelligent explanation. But how important to know that moral habits are as instinctive as any others! When men carefully cultivate the heart they more easily see and do those things that are right. The longer a man has lived a truthful, upright, useful life, the stronger reasons has the world to believe that he will never depart from this; the longer a man goes on in evil, the more easily he justifies his course, finds his pleasures in it, and sees no sufficient reason for desiring any change. Habits of evil tend strongly to perpetuate themselves.

Every man sets himself in array against his own best interests when he enters upon any degrading course. It is very far from being true that every man is willing to do good to himself. When men get entangled in any course, they become habituated to it, they see very imperfectly the benefit of any change, they are loth to make any effort to effect it. Go to any ignorant man who is unable to read a word, and who has been living in this way for many years, yet he does not realize the degradation of his ignorance, nor prize the boon of knowledge nor care to strive for its possession. It is just so with righteousness. Men in love with sin have no eyes to see its beauty. Men who love lying see not the excellency of truth, men who make a gain of fraud set no proper value upon integrity, and men of impure thoughts are incapable of respecting purity. In all such the moral perceptions are blunted; you might just as well expect delicate sensitiveness in a hand hardened by toil, or keen vision in a half-blinded eye, as just moral discernment in such a heart. Indeed men often go far on in a career of evil entirely unconscious of the serious nature of the change wrought in them, until they compare what they are with what they were long since, and see the sad decline.

It is unhappily too true that the course of this world tends to keep a man still in the way of evil he has unhappily chosen. Men form habits very often without much reflection; and habits of sin grow as fast and are as hard to break, to say the least of them, as any others. Much of human evil is due to our social nature, and men easily fall in with the habits of their companions. How many who have been trained from their childhood to love the sanctuary are thrown into circumstances that lead them to abandon their earlier practice! They fall in with associates whose habits correspond to this, and they thus gradually separate themselves from the elevating tendencies of the house of God. Under the influence of this social feeling the hands of men are often strengthened for evil from which otherwise they might shrink; and sometimes indeed, with conscience enough to feel an occasional sense of degradation, they maintain a character for themselves, and they raise up their children in a style of life widely different from their own early training and their own early thoughts. And these things are not only true of men and families that fall low in the social scale through profligacy, drunkenness or sensuality. It is easy to see how hardened, how wretched, how hopeless are some persons in all our communities whose youthful prospects were bright, whose progress has been gradually downward, yet who laugh now at all attempts to compassionate or reform. Alas! in these days of fast living the career of sin is often rapid. Many a young man among us of respectable and even godly parentage is, far beyond his years, an adept in sinful arts; loves the social glass, the billiard-table, the place of more disreputable vice; knows well the language of profanity, scoffs at serious things and derides the thought of his subjection to the gospel of Christ. And yet the years are very few since he was a child in the Sabbath-school, singing the songs of Zion and reading the lessons of the great Master; and had any Elisha then lifted the veil of futurity and shown him a picture of what he has now become, he would have said with Hazael, "Is thy servant a dog."

But there are downward changes sad and dangerous, and only more deceitful because less disreputable. The heart may grow hard in irreligion, while yet a respectable standing is maintained in society; a man may even grow in the esteem of his fellow-men while yet he is going farther and farther from his God. Advances in life of every kind are so gradually made, our opinions so gradually change, our habits are so gradually formed, that there is no shock given to the mind, as there would be if we fell down so low at one single moment. But how many live as they never thought they would! Families trained to attend the sanctuary learn to neglect it; children accustomed to family piety become parents themselves and train their offspring with no voice of prayer at the table or the household altar; men and women who once thought that the great end of life for them would be to secure the soul's salvation, now think little of this, do nothing seriously to secure it, and have before them every prospect of dying unreconciled to God. Even a prophet's voice could scarcely have persuaded them a few years ago that they would ever so feel, so live, so die. They flatter themselves indeed that they are no worse than others; they plead that circumstances beyond their control have led them gradually to their present standing; they perhaps still promise that they will one day change. But they cannot deny that others have served God in circumstances as trying as theirs; that the evil way of others is no justification of their ungodliness, and that the very disposition they now have to apologize for their guilt is sad proof of a heart hardened in iniquity and likely still to continue in this way of evil. Let this not be forgotten, that respectability in the eyes of man is no excuse for the guilt and folly of neglecting God, and that the loss of the soul must result from inattention to personal religion.

We all know that the progress of the human mind in sin may go on till all sense of shame is lost, till God in his long-suffering is wearied out and has given the sinner up, till there is no hope of reformation, till reason and Scripture agree to forewarn us that the guilty man will remain a sinner for ever. What a fearful sentence is that on the last page of God's word, and declaring the final experience of men's sin!—"He which is filthy, let him be filthy still." Let us not attempt to sketch either the characters or the doom of such. Suffice it to say that among these enemies of God and of their own souls are thousands who never dreamed of living so, who had prospects and made promises as fair as any of us, who flattered themselves that the current of sin should not carry them to the dark gulf of perdition. And a few years hence strange things will be true of many who now think quite otherwise: they are neglecting interests that cannot safely be neglected; they are indulging delays that are ensnaring; they are playing with engagements that delude the soul; and if even they escape the gross and disreputable vices which bring ruin and disgrace upon so many, they may go far enough to meet that irreparable loss—the perdition of the soul.

Is there no remedy for these dangers to which we go forward in life? Is there no way for the guilty man to stop, even after he has been entangled, and find a better, safer, holier path? There is, but it is not the way of man. Above man must we look for teachings, for strength, for guidance in the new paths of duty and of life eternal. The only safeguard against evil for this world and the next is a humble faith in the gospel of Jesus Christ: his blood purges from our iniquities past; his Spirit renews our minds to the love of holiness, guides our feet in ways of right, restrains our hearts in times of temptation; his providence protects those who put their confidence in him. The grace of Christ does not indeed relieve us from the constantly-occurring responsibilities of life, but it teaches us how to meet them; it does not ward off life's afflictions and calamities, but it sustains us in the endurance of them; it does not change our duties, but it quickens the conscience to know them, renews the heart to love them and strengthens the hand to do them. This grace of Christ forgives our sins, removes our fears, lightens our sorrows, sweetens our joys, purifies our affections, sanctifies our engagements, brightens our prospects: it is that blessing of God that makes rich, and no real sorrow is added, Prov. x. 22.

For the sake of others, every man needs this purifying grace. We cannot live and not influence those around us. Parents influence their children and husbands their wives; brothers and sisters affect each other, and friend influences friend; and all this has its inevitable bearing upon the immortal life. For every man influences others according to his own character, and not differently from what he himself is.

For the sake of his own soul, let every sinful man seek the renewing grace of Christ. It is impossible to calculate how far away indulged evil may carry any man. It is Niagara's current that cannot be controlled by oars and sails. Every onward movement increases the peril. Like Hazael, you may think that you can never become so vile. Yet you do not know even now how far from God you have already gone, how near to a more dreadful fall your feet already stand, or how much like your present thoughts were the thoughts of many who have long since perished. To stop now is wisdom. Promises are deceitful; halfway measures are vain; every moment of lost time is a loss; and though possibly to delay a little longer may not be fatal, it is foolish and dangerous. It is the duty, the privilege, the safety of every sinner to fear now the dangerous paths of evil, and to fly now to the pardon Christ gives and the duties Christ commands.

CHAPTER XV.

JUDGMENTS UPON THE HOUSE OF AHAB.

IT is lamentable to see at this period of Jewish history how great was the influence of the wicked house of Ahab upon both the kingdoms into which the nation was divided. The two thrones were united by marriage: a daughter of the Sidonian Jezebel was the wife of the son of good King Jehoshaphat; so now Ahab's son Jehoram wore the crown of Israel, and his grandson, Ahaziah, wore the crown of Judah. We may expect therefore to see the bitter fruits in both lands of those iniquities which God's prophets for twenty-five years have so boldly rebuked. It is likely that the solemn words of Elijah and Elisha have done much to prepare the way for the destruction of the house of Ahab; but the unsettled state of the kingdom, which owed its origin to rebellion, and which had already seen so many sudden and bloody revolutions, the want of any permanent sentiment of loyalty among a people that had been ninety years governed by a series of upstart usurpers, and the desolating cruelties of the reigning family,—all tended to prepare the people to throw off easily the yoke of Ahab's house. How could there be happiness in Israel, since the people could not forget the public and private injuries inflicted by this haughty royal family, when so many cherished sentiments of religion had been grossly outraged, when the best men of the land had been wantonly slaughtered, when the judgments of God had been so severely felt for the sins of the people? The stern vigilance of a military king and the cruel intolerance of a heathen queen might suppress the murmurs of the people; the power may have seemed strong in energetic hands; and Jezebel may have dwelt in Jezreel as secure as she was proud. But the calm was deceitful. A storm was ready now to burst, and the strong towers which the foolish man Ahab had built upon the sand were soon to be in ruins. If Jezebel could dwell hard by the vineyard of Naboth and forget him, the people neither forgot her crime nor Elijah's words for its avenging. If she and her son dwelt secure in a palace of ivory (1 Kings xxii. 39; Amos iii. 15), the miseries of an oppressed people in contrast with this splendour are preparing to cast down their pride. The providence of God had so prepared for the fulfilment of his word that an easy accomplishment attends the prophet's bidding; and, like a gleam of lightning from a cloudless sky, the bolt falls for the destruction of Ahab's house for ever.

Another war had sprung up between Israel and Syria, and a great battle had just been fought at

Ramoth-Gilead. In the days of Ahab this important fortress was in the hands of the Syrians, and that king lost his life in the vain attempt to recover it. As the combined forces of Israel and Judah had been defeated there, it may have been mortifying to both the kingdoms that now, after fourteen years, the Syrians still held the town; and so we read that both the kings joined their armies to make another attack upon it. We are not informed whether victory or defeat resulted; we only know that, as in the first battle Ahab was killed, so in this second his son was wounded, and that the forces of Israel were not completely routed. There is one verse that seems to say that the town was taken, 2 Kings ix. 14. The king was so wounded that he was carried to Jezreel, where Ahab had built a palace "hard by" the fatal ground of Naboth, that he might recover, and Jehu, his chief general, either still continued the siege about the city, or held the city itself. We incline to think that the attack in which the king was wounded was successful, and that Jehu was left to keep the city when Jehoram retired. The king of Judah, allied by relationship and in arms, came also to Jezreel to see the convalescent king of Israel; and thus Judah was made to share the bitter fruits which God gave to all who were joined in Ahab's iniquities.

Elisha called a young man of the sons of the prophets and sent him upon an important errand to the camp at Ramoth-Gilead. Perhaps he sent because he himself could not go. It was important that no man should know the errand of the messenger; that no conjecture of the coming changes should be made in the land; that the reigning family should be taken wholly by surprise, and thus the taking of innocent blood be spared. Elisha was too well known in Israel to allow that he should journey toward the camp from which the king was absent. Immediate conjectures would spread abroad of the prophet's design, and the words of Elijah were too well remembered to make the interpretation of Elisha's visit favourable to the present king. An unsuspected messenger, therefore, is sent to fulfil at length the long-delayed duty which God had laid upon Elijah in the deserts of Sinai twenty years before: "Jehu the son of Nimshi shalt thou anoint to be king over Israel," 1 Kings xix. 16. The words of God may seem to delay, yet find they always their sure fulfilment. The young man, though perhaps clothed as a prophet, passed unsuspected through the land, and reached the camp of Israel. It may be that his office gave him easy access to the commanders; these he found gathered together, but he called Jehu aside privately, that he might make known the commission of Elisha. Jehu went with him into a private apartment; and there the young man solemnly broke the significant flask of oil, poured it upon his head, and in the great name of Jehovah, the true God of Israel, anointed him to be king of the land! He then gave him a solemn charge to destroy the wicked house of Ahab, and reminded him of the words of Elijah, which Jehu himself had heard from the prophet's lips so many years before. Having fulfilled his errand, the young prophet opened the door and hastily fled. His part was accomplished; the other steps to overthrow the reigning family must be taken by Jehu himself, and by the army which was doubtless ready to throw off an oppressive yoke.

When Jehu returned to his associates their curiosity was awakened to know the meaning of this visit. They called the prophet a mad fellow, either because the prophets of Baal, with whom they may have confounded him, were accustomed to rave after the manner of heathenism everywhere, or because men in all ages give the name of madness to the warmth of true religious feeling. Even when Paul spoke but the words of truth and soberness, he was accused as one beside himself, whom much learning had made mad. Perhaps Jehu wished to gain time, that he might sound the disposition of his fellow-leaders before he took a step so bold as revolution. He therefore answered lightly, with the contempt of religious men that is so natural to the irreligious: Oh you know what kind of communications these prophets are wont to make! But the curiosity of the officers is not so easily allayed. They know at once that Jehu is concealing the matter; this was no visit to speak simply of religious duties; perhaps they saw the traces of the anointing oil upon Jehu's head, or noticed in his manner that something extraordinary had occurred. Then Jehu told them that by Jehovah's authority he had been anointed king over Israel. Not a word of opposition was spoken, but with joyful alacrity the captains hastened to transfer their allegiance to Jehu, and before all the army to proclaim him king. They spread their garments on the earth, that in token of his new dignity he might walk upon them; they set him up upon a high place, that all in the camp might see; and with the sound of the trumpet they declared him king in the land. Let us not say that in this revolution the crown was easily transferred from one head to another. Everything that can justify a revolution in any government belongs to this sudden change of dynasty in Israel. This thing was done by the express command of God, whose it is to put down one king and to exalt another. Apart from this, all the ordinary indications which determine the approval of Providence to the changes of earthly governments may here easily be marked. This kingdom of Israel, be it remembered, began in unjustifiable rebellion, and reaped the fruits of its own wrong in ceaseless changes and revolutions up to this time. It is remarkable that, so far as we read, no king of Israel was ever anointed before Jehu. But if ever a kingdom could plead the chief argument of modern times to justify a revolution, this plea belonged to Israel under the family of Ahab. No formal declaration of independence, indeed, was issued; no recounting was made of a long train of abuses and usurpations betraying the hand of despotism; no appeal was made to the nations that a tyrannical throne had been deaf to all milder remonstrances for relief. Yet the history of Israel for nearly a century, the history of this reigning family from the days of Omri, was one long record of justice perverted, of religion corrupted and persecuted, of innocence wronged and murdered, and of the whole land made desolate by the judgments of an angry God; while the luxurious princes reposed in their palaces decorated with ivory, and while at the last a foreign queen handed down the vices of pride, imperiousness and cruelty to be for ever associated with the name of Jezebel. We need not wonder if this long preparation under princes whom no people could love has made Israel ready for the easy change of rulers.

Jehu takes his measures with promptness and prudence. Finding the army ready to support him, he gave immediate orders that no one should be allowed to leave the camp. He would have no alarm spread; he would give the family of Ahab no opportunity for either resistance or flight. Leaving, perhaps, a guard in or around Ramoth, he marched immediately upon Jezreel with a sufficient division of the army to effect his purposes, and to bring himself to Jehoram the first tidings of the revolution. The two kings of Judah and Israel—the son and the grandson of Ahab—are there together, unsuspecting their sudden doom. It was usual for kings to station a sentinel upon a tower of the royal residence to look out especially for expected tidings. Doubtless at this time they expected hourly news from the army which lay at Ramoth-Gilead. When, therefore, the watchman gave notice that he saw a body of men approaching, orders were at once made, in the king's anxiety, that a special messenger should go out and meet them and hasten back with the intelligence. Jezreel occupied the brow of a rocky eminence overlooking the valley—a magnificent site for a city—and commanding a noble view eastward to Bethlehem on the direct road to Ramoth. The sentinel on the tower could see the messenger approach the coming army, but without knowing what had occurred; could see also that he made no effort to return. Jehoram, still unsuspicious of evil, sent forth another messenger, and he also did not return. By this time the approaching bands were sufficiently near the city to enable the sentinel to decide that they were under the command of Jehu. In our rendering of the passage it says, "He driveth furiously;" and from this we are wont to call every driver a Jehu, especially one who drives rapidly or recklessly. But in this case it is worthy of notice that the Arabic version, one of the Targums and Josephus, have a reading quite the reverse. He driveth slowly and orderly; and what seems more strange, either of these opposite senses would, for different reasons, very well suit this connection. On the one hand to say he drove furiously would suit Jehu's promptness of natural character, and the necessity for rapid movements at this especial time. On the other hand, if he came up the valley in a slow and orderly manner, time would be given for the coming of the two messengers; his very order might convince the king that it was not a routed army that was falling back upon Jezreel, and the very deliberation might call forth the monarch to meet him. But, however the king was moved, it was divinely ordered that the son of Ahab should receive his death-wound where the dogs licked his father's blood—on the grounds of Naboth.

When Jehoram knew that the approaching army was led by his old commander, he ordered his chariot to be prepared, and in company with the king of Judah rode forth to meet him. Doubtless Jehu read the full success of his enterprise in the significant fact that the meeting-spot was in the vineyard of Naboth. His first words in answer to the king's demand reveal his whole purpose, and Jehoram made a hasty effort to escape. It is worthy of our notice that the idolatries and witchcraft of Jezebel are put forth as the great cause of the public discontents and the justification of all that Jehu had now done. There were other reasons truly, but partly because Jehu himself was not prepared to correct all the evils under which the land had so long groaned, and partly because nothing was more prominent or more insufferable than the imperious rule of Jezebel—who remained in full influence and power through the reigns of two kings after the death of her husband—Jehu needs only now say that her wicked rule could no longer be borne. Nor could Jehoram escape. Jehu himself drew a bow with his full strength and sent the fatal arrow through his heart with instant effect. The Bidkar here mentioned was perhaps the captain of Jehoram's chariots. When the chariot stopped on the death of the king, Jehu addressed him as a familiar acquaintance, and reminded him that sixteen years before they two had rode together on this very spot by the side of King Ahab, when they met the stern form of Elijah the Tishbite; that they both had heard the weighty words then spoken of the royal house, and that they were both now witnesses to the fulfilment of divine justice upon its iniquity. Ahab indeed had humbled himself and put on sackcloth at the prophet's word, and God had declared that the evil should come in his son's days, 1 Kings xxi. 27–29. And now that the time had arrived, let the carcass of Jehoram be cast upon the vineyard for which Naboth's blood was unjustly shed, and without burial, let the fowls of the air eat his flesh.

In the mean time, Ahaziah, the king of Judah,

nearly made his escape. He turned his chariot at the cry of Jehoram, and fled hastily over the great plain of Esdraelon: in another part of the Scriptures we are told that he hid himself in Samaria (2 Chron. xxii. 9), which doubtless means in the kingdom, not in the city of the name; but he was overtaken at Gar and wounded there, and finally put to death by Jehu at Jezreel. It is likely that these things occurred a few days later, but they are briefly recorded here as a part of Jehu's energetic measures. If the king of Judah had remained at home, it is likely that Jehu would not have molested him. But his coming was providentially ordered that, as he was of the kindred of Ahab and shared his crimes, he might partake of the judgment denounced upon that house, 2 Chron. xxii. 7. So afterward certain brethren of Ahaziah fell also under the sword of Jehu, 2 Kings x. 13, 14; though he made no attempt to destroy Athaliah, who kept herself within the bounds of Judah. For the sake of his paternal grandfather, Jehoshaphat, who was one of the good kings of Judah, the body of King Ahaziah was allowed burial, and his people brought him to Jerusalem and laid him in the sepulchre of his fathers. Compare 2 Kings ix. 28; 2 Chron. xxii. 9.

But the work of Jehu is not accomplished, though the king has fallen beneath his fatal arrow. The chief enemy of Israel's prosperity yet survives. The name of Jezebel had been a terror for more than thirty years to all who had dared to resist her bidding, and it remains to be seen whether her energy cannot still organize a fierce resistance. And we have every evidence that she failed to withstand Jehu not for want of will. A king's daughter, a king's wife, the mother of two kings and the grandmother of Judah's monarch, Jezebel disdains to turn her back upon a foe who now at length she has no power to conquer. Whether she could have made her escape by flight we do not know, but she used the precious time for other purposes, and gives evidence that her thoughts were not at all in that direction. We could admire the boldness and resolution of Jezebel if it was but shown in any good cause, but there is a curse pronounced in God's unchanging word for those who call evil good, who put bitter for sweet, who put darkness for light. Let us learn from her that the natural tendency of pride is to grow more proud, of rebellion against God to grow more rebellious, of a hardened heart to be still more obdurate; and let us not wonder that the enemy of God and God's people, through so many cruel years, shows no tokens of penitence at the last. Jezebel is ready to die as she has lived, but there is wickedness as fearful in the final obduracy of her impenitence as in any earlier scene of her imperious life. The last days of the wicked may be variously spent; they may be tormented before their time, or they may have no bands in their death; but let every wise man join in the solemn prayer of David, for death and for eternity, "Gather not my soul with sinners!"

When Jezebel heard the tidings of the defection of the army and the death of her son, she neither mourned his death nor sought to escape her own. Aware that she had no forces to avenge her son, she resolved to court and brave the end that now drew nigh. She immediately made her toilet in the most magnificent manner of the Oriental ladies. The fashions of a foreign land, and even of different times in the same land, seem ridiculous to those who do not use them.* Let us not think that at Jezebel's age she attempted to brighten her beauty and thus make a favourable impression upon the new conqueror. She thought of nothing of this kind. Her entire design was to express her contempt and defiance toward a man who had been raised to the highest office in the kingdom, and had returned ingratitude to those who had exalted him. Instead of hiding in the recesses of the palace, she

*The fashion of painting the eyes—*i. e.*, the *eyelids*—is described ridiculously enough by Dr. Kitto in his Biblical Illustrations, as reminding one of "a chimney-sweeper who had cleansed his face as well as he could, but had not succeeded in cleaning the soot from his eyelids." Yet this is just the description given by Juvenal of the fashion among the fops he berates in Rome: "This fellow with an oblique needle makes his eyebrows long with the moistened stibium (soot), and raising the lashes paints the quivering eyes." Sat. ii. 93–95. See the whole matter explained, with cuts of the painted eye and the instruments used, in Dr. Thomson's The Land and the Book, ii. 184.

came as a queen to the open window, and as the victorious Jehu came in triumph through the open gates, she boldly reminded him that an Israelite of former days had conspired against the throne, had slain the king, and after an inglorious reign of a week had been burned with fire in the palace of his usurpation. Perhaps she thought that this might be the rallying-cry for a reaction among the hosts of Jehu: "Had Zimri peace, who slew his master?" But Jehu's boldness is a match for her own. He could have told her that Zimri was not, as he was, the captain of the army, and that the title of Omri—her own predecessor—lay, like Jehu's, in his sword. Yet if Jezebel hoped for help among his followers, Jehu defeated her with her own weapons. He called back to the window where she stood that those who were disposed to secure his favour should cast her down. This is the necessary penalty of tyranny, that the attendants of a tyrant have no warm attachments to the tyrant's person. When the authority of Jezebel is evidently ended, her own chamberlains are ready to lay violent hands upon her. They cast her down at the very gateway of the palace, and the horse-hoofs and the chariot-wheels of the triumphant cavalcade trod her under foot with that horrible indifference so easily learned upon the fields of war.

Jehu celebrated his ascension to the throne with a royal feast in the palace of Ahab. Though he was a weapon in the hands of the Almighty to execute his just wrath upon that ungodly family, there is little in the new king to call forth our approbation. Only a grade less evil than the family he supplanted, he may remind us that revolutions among a godless people often leave still existing the chief evils, that can be removed by no national changes less than a national repentance. In the midst of his unfinished work, Jehu shows himself the unfeeling executioner; calling us, it may be, to notice that a more tender-hearted man than he might in that very thing have been unfit to punish the iniquities of such a land and family. If these records seem painful, more dreadful still are the crimes that called such judgments down; and deeply seated was the gangrene in Israel when the sword of so rude a surgeon could not cut it out. The unfeeling Jehu eats quietly in the banquetting-chambers of Jezreel, while she who built these halls and reigned there so long in splendour lies a neglected corpse upon the pavement of the court. If anything can be more shocking than the narrative of Jezebel's end, which the lips of Elijah had so long before announced, it is the testimony of travellers that we have here a record of no uncommon scene in Oriental lands. Troops of wild dogs, whom no man owns or feeds, prowl around the cities of the East, and speedily devour every portion of flesh left where they can find it. And many travellers agree to say that the bottoms of the feet and the inside of the hands are the only portions of the human body which these animals always leave untouched. The words of Elijah were fulfilled concerning Jezebel by the wall of Jezreel.

These dreadful. scenes in Israel give serious warning to all succeeding ages to watch the growth of evil principles among any people; to recognize the certainty of divine judgments for national sins and the growth of judgments from sins; to call peoples and individuals to repentance before that high authority that cannot be resisted and will not be mocked; and indeed to prevent the common flatteries of man's deceitful heart that prosperous providences give any token of the sinner's final impunity. Less than a century before this time, when the kingdom of the ten tribes had separated from the throne of David, their new king Jeroboam, through political expediency, had led his subjects into idolatry. No direct attempt was made to repeal the Mosaic statutes, even when a principle directly subversive of their essential excellence was introduced; the people were allowed nominally tô worship the God of their fathers, yet they bowed down before the golden calves. Against these new doctrines a protest was raised by many faithful men among the ten tribes; and these, and especially the Levites, separated themselves from the kingdom and took refuge with their brethren in the land of Judah, 2 Chron. xi. 13–17. It was a great injury to Israel when thus the best men of the land were proscribed for their religion's sake and driven to find a home elsewhere. This mad policy has found its imitators in modern Europe; nor is it too much to say that when France slaughtered and drove forth the Huguenots, she helped to lay the foundation of England's greatness and prepared the way for her own desolations. The industry of that people would have given their native land the pre-eminence in European manufactures and commerce; their patriotism would have saved her from many a disastrous reverse; their piety might have prevented the fearful outbreak of infidelity and the horrors of the Reign of Terror. Jeroboam's folly early planted in the kingdom of Israel the seeds of mischief and dissolution. It was a land of revolutions. Three kings out of five had perished by violence before Omri, the father of Ahab; and now this new dynasty was overthrown by another as soon to perish. The growth of evil is manifest. The great sin of Jeroboam, the son of Nebat, is ever mentioned with abhorrence in the sacred narrative; but even this was a light matter for the house of Ahab, and they excelled in wickedness all that had gone before them. Yet could not Ahab have suddenly brought in the abominations of the Sidonians? Jeroboam prepared his way, a corrupted people were prepared to become more corrupt, and every new evil tended to bring in greater iniquities.

And well should Israel have known that the

judgments upon the land were the tokens of the Lord's anger against them. The prophets of God, many times at the peril of their own lives, and sometimes to the endurance of fatal persecutions,* gave express warnings in the very face of their kings; and from the death of Jeroboam's lovely son to the final catstrophe of Jezebel, the words of God's prophets found their alarming fulfilment. And indeed the judgments sprang so forth from their sins, and were so closely connected with them, that blinded eyes alone could fail to see whence these troubles all came. If they worshipped the sun under the name of Baal, their own chosen divinity was allowed to shine for three years with all his strength upon their fields, unbroken by the shadow of a cloud, unmoistened by dew or rain; yet would not Israel learn the folly of putting one creature in the place of Him who made them all. If Ahab coveted the fields of Naboth, who could not see the just reward of his crime when the avenging soil was moistened with his blood?

How vain was kingly authority to stay the march of Providence that so strangely rules by all and over all! In all these scenes of folly and madness in Israel, we see the full play of men's way-

* Dr. John Owen says that Babylon was the first state in the world that ever persecuted for religion. He must have thought too leniently of the severities of Egypt, overlooked the proscription of Jeroboam, and forgotten that "Jezebel slew the prophets of the Lord." Owen's Works, ix. 4.

ward passions; we see one wicked power dash in anger against another; we see apparent prosperity attend for years those who fight against God and his people; yet we see changes sudden and wholly unlooked for; we see that God never once loses his control over either good or evil; that he finds means to save or to destroy at his opportune time, and that no word from his lips fails of its due fulfilment. We wonder indeed that then and now innocence is often oppressed and vice often triumphant. Yet the innocent blood of Naboth can afford to wait the few brief years while his oppressor still reigns in Samaria, for the day hastens when the dogs shall lick the blood of Ahab. The martyred prophets could better afford to die than Jezebel to live, for they rested from their labours, and she went on to fill the cup of her iniquities, whose bitter dregs she must yet wring out and drink. The divine forbearance is indeed marked in all these records of Israel, especially that such prophets as Elijah and Elisha bore testimony so plain and through so many years; but this all marks more clearly the sin of the land, and justifies the increasing calamities, which, after another century of troubled annals, ended in the dissolution of the kingdom, and in such a captivity of the ten tribes that their very place remains unknown even down to our own times.

As no nation, so no individual, can mock this mighty God. Few names are recorded of all the children of men with greater abhorrence than that of Jezebel; few have her opportunities, few indeed her abilities, for doing good or evil. What good might this Sidonian princess have wrought in Israel had her energy, resolution, zeal and tenacity of purpose been used for the good of the people! The liberality that fed so many prophets of Baal might have re-established the worship of Jehovah; the zeal that slew the Lord's prophets might have extirpated idolatry; the energy that appalled and oppressed Israel might have raised it to the first rank of the kingdoms around it. The misdirected efforts of the human mind, how have they cursed the earth they should have blessed, scattered what they should have gathered, cast down what they should have built up! And just here lies the unavoidable responsibilities of every living soul, to use well the abilities and opportunities providentially belonging to each. And men do use in some directions the powers God has given them. They learn, yet are often ignorant of the most important knowledge, lying too within their reach. They love, yet their affections are grovelling, and the heart fixes not on God, its only proper object. They do, but it is the service of self and not of God. If men would but give religion the same time, the same interest, the same zeal which they give to other things, they would no longer rob themselves of life and hasten on to find the fearful end of all their delusions. They live in flattery, to die in delusion or despair. Many who are not the imitators of Jezebel's wickedness are still strangers to God and holiness. Few have her talents; few her influence; few her miserable end. But many abuse all the talents they have, live without salutary influence, and die as she did—at least in this respect, that upon their sinful heads come the just judgments of God.

CHAPTER XVI

THE INIQUITY AND RUIN OF AHAB'S HOUSE.

WE may well notice how great a change can be briefly made when God's time has come to destroy the wicked. A century before the days of Jehu, David had sung, "I have seen the wicked in great power, and spreading himself like a green bay tree; yet he passed away and lo he was not; I sought him, but he could not be found," Ps. xxvii. 35, 36. And now a new fulfilment of his words takes place in another generation, and for the instruction of all ages. The family of Ahab suddenly disappears from among men. Just now they seemed in great power; spreading themselves like a bay tree *i e.*, a tree in its native soil—one that had never been stayed in its growth by transplanting. Jezebel was indeed a foreigner, but she grew strong *like* a bay tree. If any one had judged from appearances of Ahab's house, they would have said that the fulfilment of Elijah's words were wholly improbable, if not impossible. The family was now stronger than ever, and had every prospect of continuance. Jezebel lived in Samaria and had entire rule over her son; Athaliah, a daughter like-minded with her mother, as we shall soon see, ruled over Judah, of which her son was king; and the posterity of Ahab, doubtless including grandchildren and even the fourth generation, and many of them very young, now numbered not less than seventy souls. There seemed little likelihood that a tree which, like the Indian fig tree, sent down its branches to take root and fill up wider territory, could be torn up by any storm.

The posterity of Ahab to the number of seventy were in the care of various persons who were bringing them up. It may be that this was another of the foreign customs introduced into Israel by Jezebel, which in the end brought its own righteous retribution. It has been customary in some Oriental countries for the king to put the cost and trouble of educating the royal family upon nobles and rich men. A child is sent into a certain household as a royal favour, to be trained there. It is a dangerous, troublesome and expensive charge, but the person so highly privileged dare not refuse. The prince must be educated according to his rank, he must be indulged in everything, and the teacher lives in constant fear that he may give offence through this troublesome privilege. It is easy to see that those charged with these burdens might for policy's sake seem attached to the house of Ahab, and yet they would have no real affection for the children thus imposed upon them—no real respect for the arbitrary authority that demanded such services. Jehu knew the state of things, and cunningly took advantage of it for his own ends. That he might not seem alone in rebelling against the constituted authorities, that others might appear to join of their own accord and not under fear of his power, he sent a message to them the very opposite of what he wished and expected. He knew they had no idea of fighting for these troublesome wards, but it suited him better to have their support to his cause apparently from their own choice. He wrote them a letter bidding them choose out a successor to Joram, and to muster their forces for battle. The result was as he expected. They readily found an excuse for throwing off the yoke of Ahab's family, and sent assurances of their submission. Nor need we wonder that they so easily obeyed when he demanded the heads of these persons. In Eastern lands human life is little valued; it is thought a small matter to take off the head of a man; and these nobles of Samaria knew as well as Jehu that the word of the Lord had declared the extinction of this wicked family. They executed his stern bidding, and, according to the custom which has many examples in Eastern lands, piled the gory heads in two pyramids on either side of the gate of Jezreel.

Jehu saw this ghastly sight as he passed forth from the city, and took occasion to exonerate himself in the eyes of the people. Perhaps he means to say that if there was any wrong in what had been done, his fault was slight, who had but slain one man—his master, a wicked man, and in open fight—as compared with these elders in the land, whose usual occupations were peaceful, and who had taken the lives of so many of innocent years and committed to their care. Rather it may be he calls the attention of the people to the divine justice in the destruction of this family: This is not my work, not the work of any one man: many of the principal men of the kingdom have taken part in it. "Ye be righteous"—*i. e.*, you, the people, are capable of forming a right judgment in reference to this entire revolution, and you may see here the fulfilment of the Lord's word by Elijah the prophet, and you may know that all he has spoken shall find its fulfilment. So he proceeded to complete his commission in the city of Jezreel, and he put to death all Ahab's officers and kindred and priests.

Proceeding from Jezreel to Samaria, Jehu met a company of men who proved to be the kindred of Ahaziah, king of Judah. They were wholly ignorant of the bloody scenes that had been so suddenly enacted, and so were unprepared for any resistance. These too were all put to death to the number of forty-two. We have already given some intimation of the unhappy union of Judah with Israel at this time; we shall hereafter show how deeply that kingdom was involved in the wickedness of Ahab's family, and how just were these judgments as extended to them.

As Jehu went forward, he met with Jonadab the son of Rechab. Because an interesting account is given of this man in Jer. xxxv., we may here say a few things of him. He seems to have been a descendant of Hobab, the Kenite, into whose family Moses was married. When Hobab visited Moses in the wilderness, he invited him to take up his abode in Israel, Num. x. 29: "Come thou with us and we will do thee good." This invitation was declined at that time, yet afterward accepted, and so we read of the Kenites dwelling among the children of Israel, Judg. iv. 11. Yet they kept themselves as a separate people. Perhaps there was great temptation for them to mingle with the Israelites. Especially in times when false religion abounds, the tendency is to destroy all distinctions; men become unscrupulous and hostile to ancient rules, whether they are salutary or not. Jonadab the son of Rechab seems to have been a man of integrity and influence among his own people in the days of Ahab. Seeing the danger that the utter dissoluteness of morals in Israel would affect the feeble tribe to which he belonged, he induced his people, or at least his own family, to make a solemn covenant that they would abide by the simple habits that had so long belonged to them. They bound themselves to live in tents and altogether by pasturage. This implied that they were not to sow any seed, not to build houses, not to plant vineyards, not to drink wine. This is a remarkable example of a voluntary agreement handed down to many generations to do things that were not naturally obligatory. Jonadab was doubtless influenced by motives that sought the good of his people; the times were specially dangerous, and we may believe that his efforts were successful in guarding his own children from the fearful evils that came upon Judea in the troublous times that succeeded. Perhaps he sets us an example of what a parent may accomplish who sets himself about, in times of spreading evils, to save his own household from contamination. If Jonadab, leading his family to maintain habits that might seem so much to interfere with their comfort and prosperity, was still so successful, how much might be done by those who carefully train their households in precepts of righteousness that are directly sustained by divine authority!

Nearly three hundred years after this time, long after Ahab's house and kingdom were destroyed, we find the family of Jonadab keeping this covenant still in the days of Jeremiah. So that prophet was directed to teach a lesson to Israel from their constancy. He was directed to offer the children of Jonadab wine to drink; not, indeed, that they might drink it, but that they might refuse it. This they at once did, and gave as a reason that Jonadab had commanded them not to do so, and they had always obeyed. The prophet, therefore, was directed to rebuke the people of Israel; for though the sons of Rechab had strictly kept their father's command, yet Israel had been disobedient to God's plain and holy biddings, though repeatedly urged upon them by his prophets. And in token of the divine approval upon their filial obedience, the Lord declared that "Jonadab the son of Rechab shall not want a man to stand before me for ever." We do not know that this promise should be interpreted as if the family should never become extinct, but it explicitly declares the divine approval upon their filial piety. But it is asserted by various modern travellers that there is a band of Bedouin Arabs in the vicinity of Mecca who claim now to be the descendants of Jonadab the son of Rechab. "To this moment they drink no wine, and have neither vineyard nor field nor seed, but dwell like Arabs in tents, and are wandering nomads. They believe and observe the law of Moses by tradition, but are not in possession of the written law." The missionary, Joseph Wolff, gives an account of them in his journal; and Dr. Kitto in his Bible Illustrations gives an historical exhibit of the various mention made of this singular people by the travellers of different periods.*

Jehu met Jonadab as he passed on to Samaria. It may be that the Kenite had kept himself and his people separated from the vices of the times;

* See also mention made by Krummacher in his Last Days of Elisha; and Horne's Introduction, part iii., ch. 2, § vi., with the references there made.

and now that the Lord has raised up a reformer, he gladly comes forth to salute and congratulate him. On the other hand, Jehu rejoices to have the support of an honourable man, possessing the influence of Jonadab, and welcomes him to ride with him in his chariot. When he found that he sympathized with his enterprise, he promised that he should see his zeal to restore the worship of Jehovah. All zeal is not pure, even when it accomplishes the divine purposes. Jehu destroyed the house of Ahab and the worship of Baal, yet he did not restore the true worship of God in the land.

No sooner was the new king firmly seated on the throne with all authority in his hands than he devised a plan to extirpate the worship which Jezebel had introduced. If his heart had been right before God, he would have put down all the idolatry of Israel. But his was a zeal to build up his own power, and so it was bitter against the forms of religion that Jezebel had especially promoted. To accomplish his purpose the more effectually he resorted to stratagem and deceit. He gave out that he intended to be more zealous for Baal than even Ahab had been. We wonder that he could lead the people to trust in him after the severe measures already adopted; but it may be that while the chief captain of Ahab's armies he had shown a great zeal for Baal, so the priests of that god may have thought that new triumphs were reserved for them. He made therefore a proclamation that he intended a great feast for Baal, and enjoined all the worshippers of Baal to be present. We cannot understand that all the people who conformed to this worship either could be gathered into one temple or would be slaughtered by the severest edict. The king rather desired, as we suppose, to strike such a blow at the principal men—especially the priests of this god—as would extirpate this idolatry from the land. It is quite likely that this was a movement adapted to make the new government popular among the people. The worship of Baal was a burdensome yoke upon the people of Israel. Two classes of priests served at his altars: *First*, foreign priests brought in by Jezebel from her native dominions, and exhibiting all that pride and insolence and severity which belong to such a class upheld by the power of the government, having no true sympathy with the people about them. *Secondly*, priests raised up in Israel, who served Baal because thus they secured the favour and maintenance shown by Jezebel; and it is in the very nature of things, that such a class bear contemptible characters and are the objects of the popular hatred. And her many calamities for a generation back had come upon the land through this Sidonian worship! Now that the authority was transferred to other hands, it was easy to turn the tide of popular feeling, and if the chief supporters of this faith could but be stricken down, it would be an easy matter to cast it out of Israel for ever.

When the multitude of Baal's worshippers had gathered in the temple so that they completely filled the house, Jehu ordered that clothing—or it may be badges—should be provided for them all. Even this was taken as a mark of honour by the deluded crowd, who knew not that they were thus marked for the slaughter. After all his arrangements were completed, Jehu commanded the utter destruction of the worshippers of Baal. We will not enlarge upon this scene. As they had, so long ago, destroyed the Lord's prophets, so now were they themselves destroyed. The worship of Baal never revived after this in Israel. The great work of Elijah was now complete. Yet indeed Jehu did not return to the Lord. He revived the worship instituted by the first king of Israel, and served the golden calves. So the land still suffered the displeasure of Jehovah. The Syrians still had war with them. And God declared that the family of Jehu should sit on the throne but four generations, because he did the Lord's will so imperfectly.

In order that we may more fully understand the iniquity of Ahab's family, we must take some notice of the state of things in the neighbouring kingdom of Judah. We have before noticed that a daughter of Ahab and Jezebel had been married to Jehoram the son of Jehoshaphat, king of Judah. It would be hard to find in all history a better illustration of the old proverb, "As is the mother, so is the daughter." There was the strongest likeness between this woman and her mother: had she but been called after her, as she had her character, she might well be named Jezebel the Second. So the Scriptures call her, "Athaliah, that wicked woman," 2 Chron. xxiv. 7. Her husband must have been a mere boy at the time of his marriage; for though he had several wives, his youngest son was but eighteen years younger than himself, 2 Kings viii. 17–26; 2 Chron. xxi. 17.* It is evident that Jehoram was completely under the influence of this daughter of Jezebel. Perhaps through her ambitious longings his father was induced to associate Jehoram with him upon the throne; but when he came to reign alone his reign was crowded full of iniquities, plainly showing her power over him. His other brothers had received from Jehoshaphat presents, in money and the command of various fortified towns, but no sooner was Jehoram sole king than he put all his own brothers to death, together with various other princes of Judah. He seems in every way to have been a depraved and unprincipled man. He did not perhaps venture to interfere with the services of the temple at Jerusalem, but he led the people to worship on high places, and introduced idolatrous services, and even forced them upon the land.

And now we have the singular record that this

* The Hebrew is, "A little one of his sons." Though it seems to refer to age, it is not thought to mean decidedly the youngest. Ham is not supposed to be Noah's youngest, Gen. ix. 24.

king received a writing sent to him by Elijah the prophet, who before this time had been translated to heaven. This writing is remarkable for two things: *First,* because Elijah's ministry was usually confined to the land of Israel, but here he sends a message to the king of Judah. Yet this seems to accord well with his special ministry, since Jehoram is son-in-law to Ahab, and partakes of the sins of his house. *Secondly,* the writing is thought to be further remarkable as coming to the king after the prophet was no more upon earth. Supposing this to be so, it is possible that it had been prepared by Elijah before his translation, by the spirit of prophecy, and sent to him now in his wickedness. Elijah knew Jehoram's character, knew the influence of Athaliah upon him, and either prophetically prepared this writing in advance, or gave such a charge respecting him to Elisha that he felt authorized, even while mentioning things that occurred afterward, to send the entire message in Elijah's name. This epistle warned him of the divine judgments for his wicked departure from his father's ways. But Jehoram persisted in evil. So Edom, that had been subject to the kings of Judah, rebelled successfully against him; the Philistines and Arabians came against Judah; they seem even to have taken Jerusalem; they carried off the spoils of the king's palace, and the king's wives and children, Athaliah and her son alone escaping. About two years afterward the king died in a most miserable manner, and was indeed so detested by the people that no public mourning nor burial was made for him.

The queen, like her mother Jezebel, maintained her influence over her son, who succeeded to the throne, and was his counsellor to do wickedly. Keeping the same advisers who had gathered around his father, Ahaziah, as we have seen, kept up a close alliance with Israel, and had only reigned a single year when Jehu put him to death. And when the tidings reached Athaliah at Jerusalem that Jehu had slain all her family, had killed her brother Joram and her son Ahaziah and her mother Jezebel, had slain all the kindred of both families that were within his reach, Athaliah showed herself indeed a true daughter of Jezebel. Not a tear of sorrow glistened in her eye; not a thought of revenge seems to have stirred her soul. The single selfish sentiment of cruel ambition filled her heart. Now was the time to seize the reins of the government herself. Taking advantage of the consternation produced in Jerusalem by the sudden death of the king and of the forty-two princes of Judah whom Jehu had slain, she took immediate measures to put to death every other person that could be a claimant for the vacant throne. This daughter of Jezebel goes in this beyond anything recorded of her mother; she was willing to destroy her own helpless grandchildren to further her own ambition.

Athaliah seized the throne and held it six years—the only woman that ever reigned in Judah, and she Ahab's daughter. But God had promised that he would not utterly destroy the family of David, even though it was thus miserably allied to the house of Ahab. There was a sister of the king living in Jerusalem, by whose means the wicked purposes of Athaliah were thwarted. As Jehoram had other wives besides Athaliah, this woman was doubtless not her daughter. She bore the name of Jehosheba, and was married to the high priest Jehoiada. Somehow she managed to save the life of the infant son of King Ahaziah. Josephus says that Athaliah thought she had destroyed the whole family, and that this child was left among the slain. If he had been left for dead, it would be more easy to keep from the usurper all knowledge of his existence. So his preserver and her husband kept him in the apartments of the temple for six years, while Athaliah reigned.

At the end of that time the good priest made preparations for the coronation of the young king and the overthrow of her usurped authority. He told his secret to some of the officers in the queen's guard, doubtless well knowing whom he might trust; they entered into a solemn covenant and took an oath to support the legitimate heir to the throne; and he showed then the young king. Arrangements were made to bring him publicly before the people at a proper time. As this thing was to be done in the temple, the careful Jehoiada, to avoid all suspicion of what was going on, directed the guards to come unarmed, and found means there to supply this necessity from the spoils of David's victories that had been deposited in the house of the Lord, as trophies. When therefore the guards had been thus equipped, they took such possession of the house as to forbid all resistance. The young prince was brought forward, the crown was placed upon his head; the "testimony" was given to him—*i. e.*, he was presented with a copy of the law of the Lord, the statute-book of his kingdom—and he was exhorted to govern his people by it; he was anointed in the presence of the multitude that filled the spacious house, and joyfully hailed as king by their united voices. Perhaps few of Athaliah's friends were there, and if there were any, they dared make no opposition. The noise of their cry, "God save the king!" was heard in the palace; and Athaliah, without sending a messenger, came herself to learn the cause of the uproar. The first sight that met her eyes was that of the young king standing by a pillar of the temple with the crown royal upon his head: she needed no explanation of the entire scene, and she heard the rejoicings of manly voices and of the sound of trumpets that filled the house. She rent her royal garments and cried treason, for she knew that her hour was come. The priest would not have her slain in the temple, but ordered the guards to follow her as she hastily fled. The nearest way to the palace was perhaps the wide gateway by which chariots were wont to enter, and as she fled by this she was overtaken and slain. With her the family of Ahab disappears from history. The word of the Lord, spoken so long ago to Elijah, had now found its fulfilment.

It has been supposed by some that a trace of the divine displeasure against the house of Ahab to the third and fourth generation may be noticed in the exclusion of certain names from the genealogical record of the Messiah.* In Matt. i. 8, we read that Josaphat begat Joram and Joram begat Uzziah. But indeed three names are left out here. The true record as given in the Old Testament is, Jehoshaphat begat Joram and Joram begat Ahaziah, and Ahaziah, Joash, and Joash, Amaziah, and Amaziah, Uzziah. After the union of the house of Ahab with that of David, three generations are omitted—Ahaziah, Joash and Amaziah. Yet how great was the condescension of our Lord that such names as Thamar, Rahab and Ahab occur among his ancestors!

* Spanheim's Dubia Evangelica, i. 26.

CHAPTER XVII.

DYING SCENES AND POSTHUMOUS INFLUENCE.

THE reign of Jehu over Israel was twenty-eight years: his son Jehoahaz reigned seventeen years. During this long period of nearly half a century not a word is recorded concerning Elisha. Changing events occurred both in Israel and Judah. In Judah, things were for the better after the death of Athaliah, under the youthful Jehoash or Joash, so long as the venerable Jehoiada was still alive. The temple at Jerusalem was repaired, the consecrated things which the wicked Athaliah had perverted to the house of Baal were renewed, and the burnt-offerings, in the house of the Lord were offered continually all the days of Jehoiada. This was perhaps for a period of twenty-five years. We might judge that King Joash, so early brought under the influence of Jehoiada, so indebted to him for preserving his life and for putting him upon the throne of his fathers, and so long ready to maintain the course he pursued, would still pursue the same righteous policy when Jehoiada was no more with him. This we would the more fully expect because the laws of the kingdom required these things; the true honor and prosperity of Judah were essentially involved in them; and certainly his people and his family had lost enough already by adopting the foreign policy and principles of the wicked house of Ahab. There may have been serious defects in the influence of Jehoiada. He was a good man, and did a good work for his people and for his king. But he was already nearly or quite a hundred years old when he saved the life of his youthful sovereign; he had of course lost the energy and promptness that belong to vigorous life: we scarcely wonder to find that the youthful king needed to urge him on in repairing the temple; yet we must acknowledge that it was by no ordinary influence that he could retain his hold upon the king until he had reached the mature age of a hundred and thirty years. When Jehoiada was dead, new counsellors gathered about the king. He was now indeed old enough to choose wise plans for himself. But he did not. He hearkened to the princes of Judah, who counselled him to worship false gods. For this, wrath came upon the land, and finally a violent death upon the king himself. The Syrians, under Hazael, fought against him, and were only prevented from taking Jerusalem by a large ransom paid them out of the golden treasures of the sacred temple. The king persisted in his iniquity, though faithful prophets of God warned him of his evil way. Especially are we told that Zechariah, the son of Jehoiada the priest, to whom Joash was so deeply indebted in the exercise of his office over the people, and under the direct influence of the Spirit of God, reproved the people; and they, at the command of the king, stoned him with stones in the court of the temple and within sight of the altar where he had been their officiating priest. There seems no good reason to doubt that this is the same Zachariah whose death our Lord Jesus so solemnly charges upon the Jews. He indeed is called the son of Barachias, Matt. xxiii. 35. But as the omission of an intervening generation is very common, and as Jehoiada lived so long beyond the ordinary period of man, Zechariah, though called his son, may have been his grandson, or indeed the elder priest may have had two names—Jehoiada and Barachias. The two names are of nearly the same significance—Jehoiada, the favoured of the Lord—Barachiah, the blessed of the Lord. If the arrangement of books in the Hebrew Old Testament in the time of our Lord was the same as it is now, to name Abel and Zachariah would be to name the first and the last-mentioned martyrs (not chronologically) of sacred history.* So rapidly did Judah decline after this great crime that the king himself, helpless with disease and hated by the people, and defiled with other innocent blood, was assassinated upon his own bed, and the common detestation would not allow him to be buried in the sepulchre of the kings.

*See Ladner's Cred., i. 417.

In Israel also things went badly. Jehu took no heed to walk in the law of the Lord, and Hazael was the scourge of the land, winning victories in every quarter. After Jehu's death, his son Jehoahaz pursued the same wicked policy, and with even more mischievous results. When Hazael died, his son Benhadad succeeded to the throne of Syria, and the armies of Israel were so reduced by constant defeats that fifty cavalry and ten chariots and a body of ten thousand infantry were all that remained. The king of Syria "had destroyed them, and had made them like the dust by threshing." Yet, indeed, God was long-suffering toward this wicked people. Jehoahaz, at least in some measure, humbled himself and besought God; and he gave them such deliverance that they were not wholly subjugated. Yet still they cleaved to the sins of Jeroboam, and the worship of Astarte was still tolerated in the capital of the kingdom.

During all these eventful years we cannot think that the voice of Elisha was silent or that his influence was unfelt. But the special design of the sacred historians in their records concerning Elijah and Elisha seems to be to exhibit their faithful antagonism to the evil house of Ahab; and so no sooner did that house disappear in these troubled floods than we read little of the prophet who so long survived. Doubtless he maintained still the schools of the prophets; for, though such institutions could be kept up in such evil times only through many strugglings, a land never more needs the wholesome and important influence of a well-trained ministry than in periods of national declension and disaster. We cannot estimate the influence of a prophet of God by noticing how often his name is brought into public notice, nor even by knowing what positive good he has done. The land might have been much worse but for Elisha; fifty years of holy living and humble praying, in such a man as he, were not spent in vain, even though no earthly record was made of them; indeed, Elisha's quiet labours may have been as valuable, for the good of precious souls, as any he had previously rendered in the Church of God. When Elijah mourned over the declensions of his people, even the divine eye saw but seven thousand secret servants in Israel; now, the idolatry of Baal has disappeared with its chief promoters. Much remains undone in a land that should have been wholly devoted to God's worship; yet there is good reason to believe that many thousands of those who openly worshipped the God of their fathers might easily be found.

But the close of Elisha's labours drew nigh. There is an allotted time for earthly duties, and this past, God's faithful servants are transferred to another sphere. The Church should not wish to detain them; though we mourn their loss, we should recognize how much better it is for them to depart; and precious lessons and needed consolations may come to us from the closing scenes of the departing believer. There is, indeed, a wonderful variety in the later scenes of man's life, and this not only when we contrast the closing scenes of a believer and an unbeliever. God's eminent servants die at various ages, with their work more or less completed, and with testimony to the divine faithfulness in almost every possible form. Scarcely a greater contrast can be imagined than that which is seen in the departure from earth of these two men, who were associated together in the same work, but who were called from it so differently. Elijah, perhaps still in the vigour of his years, with his hands full of abundant toils, is met suddenly by the celestial chariots, and borne away from earth without weakness or disease or dying. Elisha lived to old age; his feeble body was emaciated by sickness; anxious friends watched by his bedside as the powers of nature gave way; death released him from his sufferings, and he was laid in the grave to see corruption. Let us look in upon his darkened chamber, for, dying or dead, Elisha the prophet yet speaks to us.

We are reminded of Elijah as we read this account of Elisha's deathbed. As the aged, feeble prophet lies in his final sickness, a splendid chariot drives up to his door, but it is not such as bore the elder prophet upward to the skies. It is but the visit of the king of Israel to see the last of a counsellor whom he and his fathers had too much neglected while he was in life. We here have also the same words which Elisha himself had used as Elijah was parted from him; but the man who utters them now is little prepared to take up the prophet's mantle. But let us not think that Elisha is every way less favoured than Elijah because the one ascends to heaven in the celestial chariots and the other dies in the weakness of a worn-out frame. An eminent preacher of the English Church* has published a discourse of great interest and power, contrasting the translation of Elijah with the death-bed of Elisha; and in this he describes Elisha as a prophet of quite superior influence, usefulness and glory. We need not decide that the younger is superior to the elder, but it is quite becoming to notice that God put different and glorious honour upon them both. It was an eminent mark of the divine favour when Elijah was translated. Not only the strangeness of this method of leaving the earth, but its excellency also, attest the divine approval of the labours and character of the servant thus distinguished. In all ages men readily confess that an especial honour was conferred upon that prophet. Yet let us not make too much of this. God did not design to put any mark of displeasure upon Elisha when he gave him not the exalted privilege he extended to Elijah, nor do his people now lack any evidence of acceptance when they also die, nor need we be surprised that very dif-

* H. Melvill. Before referred to. See chapter ii.

ferent scenes occur when believers depart. Elijah and Elisha by their different routes passed both to the same heaven; indeed, since our Lord tells us that the beggar Lazarus was carried by the angels into Abraham's bosom, why may we not judge that Elisha was borne, that every dying saint is borne, by celestial powers, not in the body and visibly, but as really, to the mansions of glory. And the time will come when everybody will be raised from the grave and will be reunited with the glorified spirit. The difference between the prophets does not pertain to matters vital; the ascension was glorious, but the deathbed was happy. And since the Lord of all the prophets—One unquestionably greater than Elijah—condescended to die, since we are able to sing,

> "The graves of all his saints he blest,
> And softened every bed,"

since his resurrection is the pledge that all his people shall rise, and since a voice from heaven says, "Write, Blessed are the dead that die in the Lord," we may devoutly recognize that God gave Elijah great honour in his translation, and yet see also that rare privileges linger around Elisha's hours of feebleness, and yet know that about many such a couch occur scenes of interest, profit and glory.

We may not only agree that the dying Elisha passed into the same heavens as safely as the translated Elijah, but that God had purposes to serve for our instruction in the very differences between their departures. There was in Elisha a trial of graces far more difficult to exercise than we can discern in Elijah. In these things men are apt to make false judgments. Sometimes a young and earnest prophet is so suddenly cut off from usefulness that men feel as if he was too ripe to stay below; so Spencer went forth in the morning in the full tide of his strength, and a wail arose at noon through the crowded city in universal grief; so many a time has the Church wondered at the early removal of those who had been well prepared for her needed service. But the infinite wisdom of God, who thus teaches his people not to rely upon an arm of flesh, gives us also the same lessons by the sorrows he lays upon servants whom yet he does not remove. So Paul languishes in a Roman prison, though so many harvest-fields lay inviting him; so John Bunyan remains a standing proof of English intolerance and of God's overruling grace; so many a noble confessor has been silenced when he would gladly speak the praise of God with unceasing tongue; so we often wonder why God so often lays a man so long aside by wasting sickness—sometimes raising men up after long months of sorrow, sometimes bidding us lay softly in the earth the emaciated frame that has through a weary sickness been racked and wasted by disease. He would bid us reflect that there are lessons of silence and suffering not less important for the great glory of God than any active zeal to promote his work. It is harder to suffer than to labour, harder to be patient than zealous, harder to exercise faith when things seem to stand still than when we see the evident progress of the Lord's work. The wisdom of God tries us when we most seem to need it, and many a prison and many a sick chamber has glorified the grace of God as truly, perhaps as acceptably, as Paul's pulpit or Elisha's chariot of fire.

We see when Elijah lies upon his deathbed somewhat of the esteem in which he is held in Israel. Matters have greatly changed in the land since Elijah passed upward. The only impression made upon Israel by the prophet's departure, though so wonderfully made, was to give joy to their idolatrous cities, and to call forth the wish that Elisha might also go. But now this prophet is better appreciated. The king himself, when he heard that Elisha was sick, hastened in his royal chariot to visit his chamber, and, recalling the heartfelt grief of Elisha at Elijah's departure, he laments over him as though the chariots and horsemen of Israel's defence were now about to be taken away. And indeed, far beyond the king of Israel's thoughts, are righteous men the strength and protection of a land. But for Elijah and Elisha far more speedy judgment had been taken on that guilty kingdom. And King Joash may remind us that evil men may hold God's servants in high esteem, may lament their removal from the community as calamities and may mourn sincerely around their graves, while yet they were very partially influenced by their best counsels. This same Joash, who wept by the prophet's dying bed, was one who maintained the sins of Jeroboam against which Elisha had all his life protested. If the servants of God could win the obedience of men to God's commands, even as much as they often secure their respect for their own personal character, we would see far larger progress made in reforming our communities. It was the unhappiness of King Joash that neither the influence of the living Elisha, nor the affecting scenes of that dying chamber, nor the gratitude due for the favours received after he was gone, had any permanent power for his good.

But the dying prophet reminds us also that God may give special usefulness to his servants in the closing hours of life. Israel was then surrounded by powerful foes, and the king's visit is made the occasion of Elisha's last public benefit. The Syrians seem to have been then in camp at Aphek, their forces arrayed against Israel. Elisha bade the king take a bow and arrow in his hands. He ought to have known—he doubtless did know, from the usages of Israel's prophets—that here was something significant of more than met the eye; yet his was a weak faith, that was half ashamed to do at all what it behooved him to do so well. Elisha put his feeble hands upon the hands of the king, bade them open the window eastward, in the direction of Syria's camp, and they shot forth the arrow of divine deliverance from Israel's foes. Why must the prophet put his hands upon the hands of the young and vigorous Joash, as if he could add strength to the king's strong right arm, or as if he was unacquainted with the use of the bow who had rule over a people that had been in continual warfare all his life? Elisha teaches a lesson which Joash never did fully learn, and which earthly warriors are still slow to believe, though taught in every age by the severest lessons of an overruling Providence. "Providence favours the strongest battalions," said the proud emperor of the French, yet he never led a nobler army than that which fell back in such disastrous retreat from the flames of the Russian capital and the frosts and snows of a Russian winter. In any age and for any contest there is no more important element of success than the blessing of God. Happy are they who seek it and depend upon it, and they who forsake this dependence forsake their own mercies. "Some trust in chariots and some in horses, but we will remember the name of the Lord our God," Ps. xx. 7. It is well enough to have a strong young monarch, but how little could Joash do without Elisha! "The trembling hands of a dying prophet, as they signified the concurrence and communication of the power of God, gave this arrow more force than the hands of the king in his full strength."* The prophet gives counsel to attack the Syrians, and gives at the same time assurance that, notwithstanding their late success, the earnest efforts of Joash should be crowned with success in a great victory at Aphek.

But the significant service is not yet ended. He bade the king take the arrows and smite upon the ground. He struck the earth three times and stopped, waiting the prophet's explanation. Alas! there was a great error here: Elisha was displeased. Had he struck the earth harder or more frequent blows, each blow would have represented a new triumph over Israel's enemies, but now only three victories were foreshadowed. Evidently Joash did not enter heartily into the prophet's measures. Perhaps he was ashamed to be guided by this feeble, dying man, as if he knew not how to shoot without Elisha; or he could see no importance in these strokes upon the earth. And indeed these were but symbols; yet a man of true faith should have recognized that man's feebleness and God's power are often brought together, that the glory may be given where it belongs. We see here that the prophet's deep interest in the welfare of his people has grown no weaker because of the body's decay: Elisha is a true patriot to the very last of life; and indeed his dying words utter his indignant remonstrance that the war is to be conducted with so little energy. We see that special usefulness be-

* M. Henry.

longs to his last hours. We have read nothing of him now for nearly half a century, but he reappears in useful influence, like an expiring lamp that flickers up into a brilliant light just as it goes out. And we should not doubt that in various ways and degrees, God's servants are often useful in the last hours of life. They may not be visited by a king nor send forth their last efforts to deliver a kingdom. But from the patient, cheerful submission of a suffering believer from the sustaining, elevating power of religious principles in times of severest trial, from the glad and bold testimony given to the divine faithfulness by dying lips, and from the earnest longings to depart and the happy anticipations of glory to be revealed, are useful influences sent forth from a sick bed, such as an active life cannot render; and feeble dying hands often shoot the arrow of the Lord's deliverance. Enemies confounded, friends strengthened, souls won to God, are not seldom tokens of the divine blessing upon the believer's latest hours. Indeed, God's people should cheerfully leave the entire ordering of their lot in his hands, since his favour may make their hours of greatest feebleness the season of most abundant usefulness; since the suffering of a sick room may teach and accomplish more than the energy of busy life; and since our dying, as the last, may also be the greatest, service done for him upon the earth.

But Elisha reminds us that death is not the last

service the dying believer renders to the world. The expiring lamp gives new light after we thought it was out. "Elisha died and they buried him." The Hebrews usually interred the dead in caverns. So the body remained still accessible after the burial was complete. When Lazarus was called forth from the grave, they needed but to take away the stone, and at Christ's commanding voice he came out. The succeeding year after the prophet's burial, a funeral procession was arrested by seeing a body of armed men approach. They had not time enough to proceed with the body to the appointed place, but the cave where Elisha slept was near at hand. So they put the man into the sepulchre of the prophet, and lo! a great wonder. The dead body no sooner touched the bones of Elisha than life returned and the man stood up. And herein is one of the marvellous excellences of the word of God—that little is said of the wonder itself: it is recorded here in the very simplest terms; we are told not one word of this man's subsequent history; we learn not a word of the influence exerted by this wonder upon the people of that day. For indeed the significance of this wonder is far beyond the efficacy it had for that man and for that time.

See in this the proof that Elisha is not beyond Elijah in proofs of divine approbation. It was a great thing to be carried upward, without dying, upon the chariots of heaven: it was a great thing, after death had left nothing of the prophet but his fleshless bones, to work still a marvel as great as any that marked his life. The two prophets teach us separate lessons. The one reveals the life to come—the glorious life when soul and body united shall be with God for ever; the other reminds us that the body, once dead, shall rise again to life. And it is interesting to notice that both these prophets together only foreshadowed, and this indeed in an inferior degree, the greatest of all the prophets —their Lord and ours. Their separate glories unite harmoniously in him. Elijah ascended—Elisha gives us an example of a resurrection. Both of these belong, in his own person, to Christ. He himself arose from the dead—arose to immortal life— and his ascension was more glorious than that of Elijah.

And this last record of Elisha's history should remind us of the influence that good men may still put forth in the earth after they are gone. In the apocryphal book of Ecclesiasticus (xlviii.) it is said of this prophet that at his death he did wonderful things—*i. e.*, wrought a great deliverance for Israel; and after his death his body prophesied. We are doubtless to understand that the divine approval given to the departed prophet would have great influence in reviving the memory of his former teachings. We have no reason to judge from this passage, or from any other in all the Bible, that the scriptural writers teach us to look for any miraculous efficacy in the relics of dead saints. We are not told here that the Israelites sought the tomb of Elisha, expecting that any such miracle would be wrought; on the contrary, their putting the dead body by his was undesigned and accidental. We are not told that they attempted to secure other benefits, having once learned what Elisha's bones might do. The people did not argue that because these bones had wrought wondrously, therefore they must receive new religious honours: no such services as kissing, touching, exhibiting, enshrining Elisha's remains were instituted; they were not adorned with silks and gold, honoured by the burning of candles nor held in adoration, nor were repeated wonders expected of them.* Modern Romanism is but little like the religion of the Bible, under either the Old or the New Testament. But this wonder wrought, not by Elisha, but by the God of Elisha, reminded the people that though the prophet died, the Lord of the prophets still lived, and that he would let fall to the ground none of the words spoken by his servants by his authority.

Death is not the last of man, even as it pertains to the earth and the men upon it. We live in the memory of others after we are gone. Every parent renews his life in his children; his neglects are fully equal to many an example directly mischievous; and his patient painstaking to bring up his family

* Chemnitz, Examen Conc. Trid., Part iv., pp. 5, 6.

in the fear of God shall bear larger and better fruit after he has gone than it did while he was yet alive. Every man exerts some influence upon those with whom he meets. How deep are the impressions we may make, how far they shall spread, it is quite impossible for any of us to say. Our responsibility lies not so much in the extent of our influence as it does in the character of it. Let us form our own characters right, do righteous deeds, speak truthful words and cherish kindly feelings, and while it is our privilege to aim at as much good as we can reach, we can better afford to be less careful touching the amount of our influence. A single cluster of sweet grapes in the Lord's vineyard is better than a loaded vine of wild and poisonous fruit.

Elisha's dead bones raised a man to life. This is the last record of his doings upon the sacred pages. Is it the last of all that he has done? Doubtless not. Elisha as a prophet of God has spoken to all succeeding generations. He is one of the long cloud of witnesses whom God has appointed to testify to the sons of men touching divine claims and human duty. The prophets do not live for ever, but the word of the Lord which which he gave to the prophets ever finds its fulfilment, and its principles remain as excellent for our teaching in these ages as when Elisha lived. Elisha has indeed lived and moved among us, for we have gone over the events of his life, we have considered the various lessons he sets before us, we have sought the only true and reasonable use of the prophet's relics, and we should now ask ourselves whether it has been any advantage to us thus to visit the grave of Elisha? The finger of God can still give power to the dead Elisha to do a thing far better than to resuscitate a lifeless corpse. The dead souls of men have often been raised to spiritual and immortal life as they have come in contact with the teachings of these ancient prophets.

We have followed this prophet from the fields where Elijah called him, through his long and useful life; we have seen that curses and blessings both flow from him, and so it has been ever since. Naaman is cured and Gehazi is smitten at the word of the same prophet. Has any one of us who have gone over these scenes in his life—who have been reminded by them of our own necessities and of the only means of cure, who have been called to fear and obey the Lord God of all the prophets—found health and life from the dead Elisha? Has any one been brought to these pages by the leadings of others, and undesignedly touched him who has lain so long in his sepulchre, like the unknown man so suddenly interrupted on his way to his grave, and received in this the gift of life? Blessed be the Lord God of Elisha, that the prophets, in a most important sense, do live for ever, and that we in these latter days may still come to their teachings, that we may find the life of our souls!

It would be a rich reward to know that our thoughts upon Elisha's life were instrumental, so long after his death, in the saving of one single soul, but for one reflection of the deepest moment. They who get not good, get damage from drawing near the prophets. Our gospel is a savour of life unto life or of death unto death, to every hearer. Elisha speaks not in the air. If we have here the teachings of divine truth, it is the guilt of man when he receives not profit from them. No minister, no evangelical writer, should be satisfied with small success. Should a physician boast of his success in saving one life, forgetful of a dozen fatal cases under the same services? Alas, the physician has the advantage of the preacher, for his patients, not ours, long as much as he for a successful issue, and use careful co-operation to that end.

THE END.

www.ingramcontent.com/pod-product-compliance
Lightning Source LLC
LaVergne TN
LVHW010224110826
845151LV00004B/1177

* 9 7 8 1 4 2 5 5 2 7 5 3 2 *